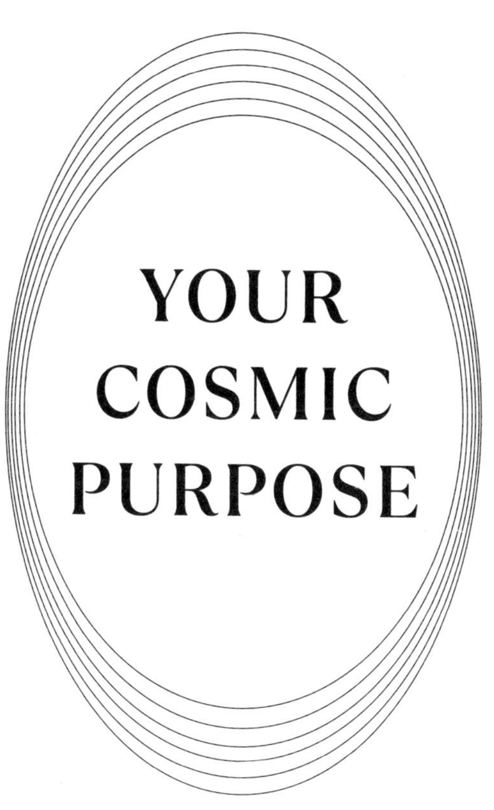

YOUR COSMIC PURPOSE

YOUR COSMIC PURPOSE

Trust in the universe and discover your life path

KIRSTY GALLAGHER

HAPPY PLACE BOOKS

UK | USA | Canada | Ireland | Australia
India | New Zealand | South Africa

Happy Place Books is part of the Penguin Random House group of companies whose addresses can be found at global.penguinrandomhouse.com

Penguin Random House UK
One Embassy Gardens, 8 Viaduct Gardens, London SW11 7BW

penguin.co.uk
global.penguinrandomhouse.com

First published by Happy Place Books in 2025

2

Typeset in 11/16pt Baskerville MT Pro by Jouve (UK), Milton Keynes

Printed and bound in Great Britain by Clays Ltd, Elcograf S.p.A.

The authorised representative in the EEA is Penguin Random House Ireland, Morrison Chambers, 32 Nassau Street, Dublin D02 YH68

A CIP catalogue record for this book is available from the British Library

ISBN 9781846047756

Penguin Random House is committed to a sustainable future for our business, our readers and our planet. This book is made from Forest Stewardship Council® certified paper.

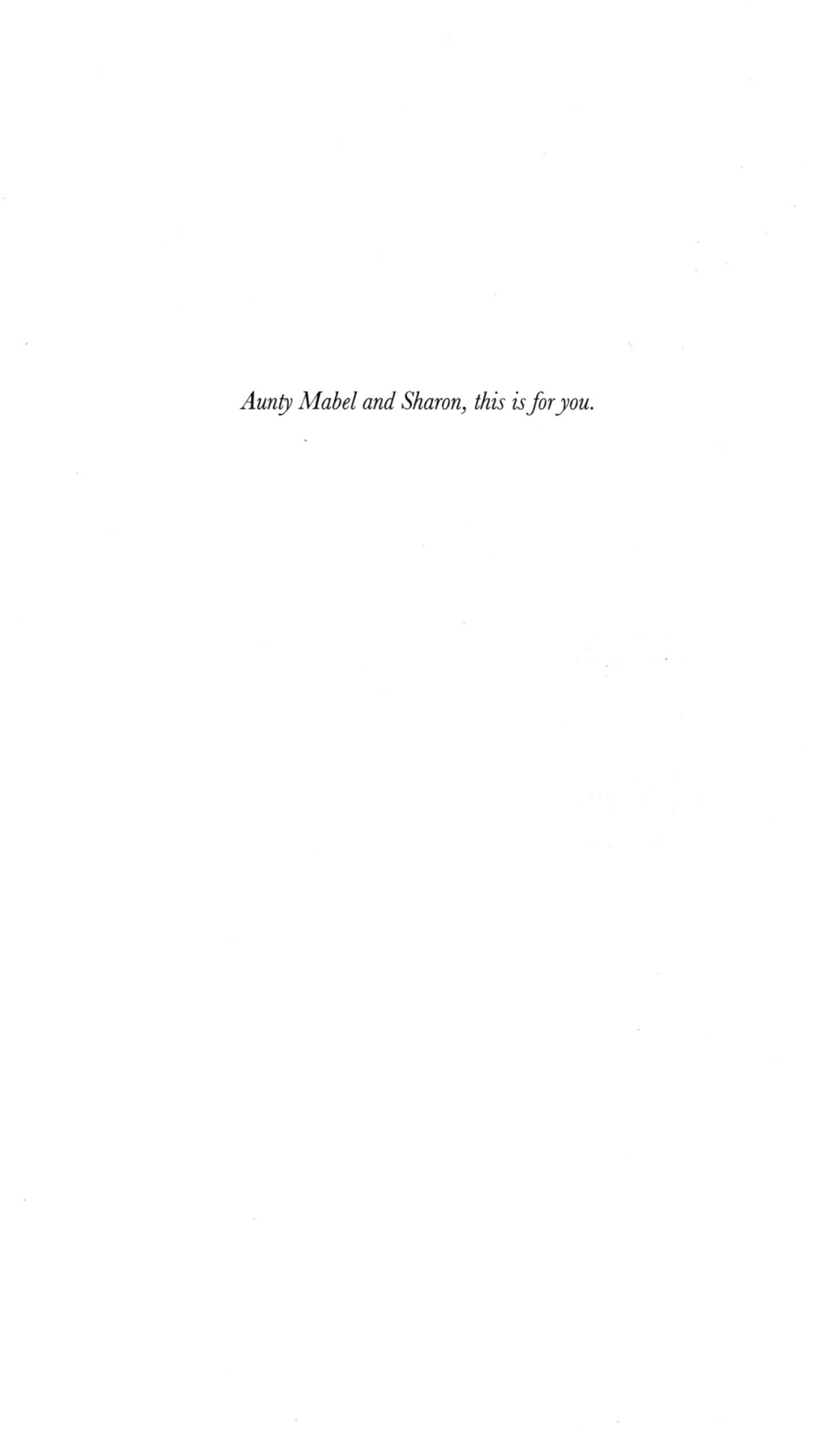

Aunty Mabel and Sharon, this is for you.

CONTENTS

INTRODUCTION

Hello, my love, and welcome on this journey towards discovering your cosmic purpose, through which you'll uncover more of who you truly are and what you're here for.

I want you to know that you've been guided to this moment; whether it was through the inner nudge you received when you heard me talk of this book which caused you to order it, a recommendation from a friend or some other means, just know that your soul led you here, to this moment . . . the beginning of this journey. Take a moment to honour that now. And, as you uncover more of your soul self as you walk through these pages with me, your soul will begin to guide you towards even more wonderful experiences and adventures that will allow your soul journey and cosmic purpose to unfold.

Let me begin by sharing a little more about my journey and what has brought me here. I've been on a spiritual journey for as long as I can remember. When I was a little girl, my great, great Aunty Mabel was one of my favourite people. She read tea leaves and tarot and was psychic, and I *adored* spending time with her. Looking back, I suppose she was my first spiritual teacher and she opened me up to a whole world outside of the physical and that which could be seen and logically understood.

I got my first astrology book when I was about 11, around the same time as I owned my first crystal, which was a tiger's eye, one of my birth stones. I remember poring over that book for days, becoming absolutely captivated by the world of astrology, and spending such a long time gazing at that crystal, fascinated that it came from the earth.

Throughout my whole childhood, I was a 'why' child and wanted to know and understand 'why' before I'd do anything! This is something that continued through my life as I sought to understand 'why', not only to the bigger questions around why we are here, but why we do anything that we do. I need to fully understand something before I can blindly follow it; I've never been one to just follow the rules. I have always had very strong intuitive and psychic senses and this knowing that there was more to life and to us and a greater source of power that we could tap into.

It's fair to say that spirituality took a sideline as I went through my late teens and discovered nightclubs, began forging a career path and started to find my place in the world, but something always niggled within me just waiting to be reawakened and re-explored when the time was right. And that time came when I met a soulmate at work in my early twenties.

He was someone I went on a real journey of self-discovery with. Together, we explored the spiritual world, travelled the physical (and astral) world and uncovered so much about ourselves and the meaning of life. I learned so many soul lessons and truths during this romantic relationship. If any of you have read *The Goddess Path*, it was him who booked me on to the course to read Goddess oracle cards, which started much of my journey with the Goddess and the Divine Feminine. Our time together was such a period of awakening my soul, deepening my spiritual practices and great growth, evolution, exploration and discovery, and then – out of nowhere – one of my best friends, Sharon, died.

Sharon was one of the greatest lights the world has ever seen. She lit up a room with her presence and her smile, and I am so grateful for our years of friendship. The moment I met her it was like I'd known her my whole life and we quickly became inseparable.

She had a young daughter, so our time together was limited to weekends, when her daughter was with her dad, or on weekdays when I'd go over to Manchester and just hang out on the sofa with her at home. We also had a Sunday ritual where I'd drive her to the supermarket to do their weekly shop as she didn't have a car.

Even doing these seemingly mundane things with her was special. She had this ability to bring so much joy into everything, even a supermarket shop on a single mum budget. She loved life, truly loved it, and even though she had been through hard times and challenges, she saw the best in everything and everyone, and made the most out of her life.

Whenever I picture her, she's always dancing (she loved to dance) with the biggest, brightest smile on her face – that's how I remember her: smiling and dancing. Which is what she was doing one of the last times I saw her, until she woke up the next morning with a bad headache and hours later was in a coma.

I remember going to see her in intensive care and telling her she needed to be better for the following weekend as we had a big weekend away planned. I was convinced she was going to be better within a few days and we'd be partying by the weekend. My mind could not even begin to accept that this was the end. But, a few days later, the phone call came – they were turning off the life support. My entire world crumbled around me. I just couldn't imagine a life without her in it.

Sharon had an open casket at her funeral and, as I placed a letter and crystal in there with her and looked at her peaceful, beautiful face, I had the huge realisation that it could have been me lying in that coffin. Any of us could leave the earth at any moment. And suddenly all the silly little things I spent so much time worrying about and all the fears and doubts that held me back and kept me stuck and stopped me from doing things seemed so irrelevant.

The church at her funeral was so packed that people were spilling outside on to the street, a testament to the number of lives she touched and how much her death became a catalyst for so much life, including mine. I made her the promise that I would continue to live for her and do all that she was no longer able to and all that I longed to do and to make her proud. My life would become a devotion to her.

I came home from her funeral, broke up with my soulmate and moved out of our home that same day. Even though the relationship was wonderful, something deep down in my soul knew that there were so many things about it that just weren't right and, after my realisation at Sharon's coffin side, I was no longer willing to live a life anything less than fully true and authentic to me.

I can't explain it, but, deep down, I knew (and had for a while, if I'm being honest) that I would never fully be able to become all I was meant to be while we were still together. We had taken each other as far as we could go, our soul contract was complete, and it was time for us to be free to embark on the next stage of our journey. I told him that as I broke up with him – that I set him free and, in doing so, I also set myself free.

And here began my real spiritual deep dive. From that point onwards, I dedicated and devoted my life to my spiritual journey and trying to understand what life was all about and what my true cosmic purpose was. I became a crystal and reiki healer, a regression therapist, an astrologer and a spiritual coach. I worked with spirit guides, angels and ascended masters, and embraced my psychic abilities. I studied meditation, energy healing and metaphysics, kabbalah, tarot and Wicca – and anything else mystical and magical that I could get my hands on. I was so hungry for knowledge and answers, and this was a time of deep soul exploration for me.

And then I found yoga. As clichéd as it sounds, I tried one class, in a local village hall, and was hooked. Yoga, with its rich, ancient philosophy, gave me an answer to every question. Through the physical practice, I was uncovering more and more layers of myself and, through the philosophy, I was connecting more to the divine consciousness.

I knew from this moment that I wanted to teach yoga. I wanted to share this life-changing practice with others, and I knew I wanted to go to India, to the source, to where yoga came from. It took me nearly two years to make this dream a reality – some of the most difficult and challenging yet beautiful years of my life. Finally, in 2009, I lived in India for a year while doing my teacher training, then taught at the yoga school I trained at while studying philosophy, pranayama and meditation.

It was here that I discovered the magic of living by the moon and immersed myself in Lunar Living, which later became the subject of my first *Sunday Times* bestselling book back in 2020. I also began my devotion and dedication to the Goddess and the Divine Feminine, and awakening my kundalini, the creative life force energy of the universe which awakens our full potential.

Upon returning to the UK, I started teaching yoga classes and workshops about living by the magic of the moon and astrology. I was one of the first people to teach yoga in the north-west of England, as it just wasn't something that was done at the time, setting up regular classes and workshops. This turned into teaching 87 sold-out retreats all over the world. I then moved to London where I started teaching corporate and private yoga classes before writing my books and moving into what I do now.

It has been a challenging, wonderful, enlightening journey so far of growth, evolution and discovery that has led me to so much purpose in sharing all that I have learned with you through social media, the Lunar Living Sisterhood, the Goddess Path Mystery School Coven and the online courses and workshops that I create.

Now I want to share it with you here, in these pages. I want to reveal what I have learned in my decades of walking this path and, in turn, help you to explore the journey of your own soul, for all our paths may be different and part of your journey is for you to discover yours.

This may be a good time for me to say that if anything I say in this book doesn't resonate with you, that's not your truth, it is more than ok. Instead, take what lands for you and leave the rest. I'm not here to teach or tell or convince you of anything. I'm here to help you to remember the depths of wisdom, knowing and truth that are already within you so that you may bring your unique cosmic purpose and message to the world.

None of us knows the definitive meaning of life, what it's all about or the ultimate spiritual truths until we once again meet our souls – if indeed you believe that is what happens when we leave the earth. It's up to each one of us to discover enough of our own cosmic purpose so that we can begin to find the answers and wisdom within us, enabling us to establish our own truths to help us live a life of meaning, purpose, spiritual connection and trust.

You discovering your own truth is a part of this journey and one that will challenge and change you. It will help you to establish deep roots in your cosmic purpose and true soul self. This was such a big part of my own journey and learnings. When I first started walking a spiritual path over two decades ago, I wanted everyone to believe what I believed. It came from a well-meaning place as it was changing my life so much that I wanted to share it with others.

But, when I looked at this more deeply, I realised it was because I didn't fully believe what I believed – I needed others to also believe it as then it must be true, and it was therefore ok for me to believe it too. So, if other people also believed that there were spirit guides, there must be, and it made it acceptable for me to believe the voices of my guides that I was hearing.

My faith was shaky to begin with, as it will likely be for you. We need lived experience to be able to fully believe in something. Initially, I would crumble or express doubt at the first sign of my beliefs being questioned or difficult things happening to me, as I couldn't understand how my soul or the universe would do that to me. But, over time, I've learned that everything is happening *for* me to help me to learn, grow and evolve, and I have established such deep spiritual beliefs that they are as much a part of me as my own hands or feet. I've experienced the divine first hand and had my beliefs confirmed to me repeatedly. They are my truth and I know them from somewhere deep within me. It doesn't matter anymore whether anyone else believes the same as me as my beliefs help me to get through hard times in life with more ease and grace, and to live a life that is (most of the time) happy, purposeful, abundant, meaningful and connected to a higher source of divine power and wisdom. This is my greatest desire for you too, and what I hope you will come to see on your spiritual journey to discover more of your cosmic purpose.

In Part 1, we uncover more about what your cosmic purpose and soul are and how you can begin a journey back to your soul self.

In Part 2, we look at practical ways you can begin to live and embody your soul and cosmic purpose to live a life that's more true to you and your life path. Throughout this part, I have included 'whispers from your soul'. These are things I would love for you to take some time with, reflect, journal and meditate on. As you go more deeply into this journey, you will be able to hear the whispers from your soul more easily as you open yourself to receiving them. You may want to get yourself a special soul journal (or even just a regular notepad or you can use the Notes app on your phone) to keep a chronicle of your journey, allowing your own soul story to unfold. It will be a wonder to look back on.

Finally, in Part 3, we look at ways you can find more of your cosmic purpose in your birth chart and astrological transits. Remember that astrology is a huge topic, so take your time getting to know your chart. I've been studying astrology for over 20 years and I still feel like I haven't scratched the surface.

Take your time with this book too, put it into practice and refer back to it often. You may want to read through it fully once and then come back to Part 2 and spend about a week with each of the concepts, diving deep and exploring them fully.

This is a journey, not a destination. I fully believe that once we 'know it all', it's time to leave the earth and return back home to soul school before coming back to earth once again. So, enjoy the journey and let your soul lead the way.

If you're ready, let's begin . . .

PART 1

WHAT IS YOUR COSMIC PURPOSE?

In this part of the book, you will learn more about how to uncover and understand your cosmic purpose and the journey that your soul takes through each lifetime as you find your way back to who you truly are.

‘There is no one
else in the entire
world like you.’

Chapter 1

WHY YOU NEED TO DISCOVER YOUR COSMIC PURPOSE

I truly believe that each and every one of us has a purpose here on earth. You came here with little seeds of your soul planted within you containing all the dreams, desires, lessons, experiences and adventures that your soul wants to go through in this lifetime to grow, evolve and awaken. In the same way that a seed contains all that it needs to grow into all that it can become, you contain within you all that you need to grow into the fullness of who you came here to be, and what your soul came here to offer to the world in the way that only you can.

There is no one else in the entire world like you.

Think about that for a moment.

In a world of nearly 8 billion people, you are completely unique. To take this a step further, it is said that the chances of you being born are 1 in 400 trillion. Yes, you read that right – 1 in 400 trillion. So many things had to happen for you to be here, from your ancestors surviving and meeting each other, to your parents meeting each other, to the exact egg and sperm meeting that created the exact DNA sequence that makes you YOU. Had another egg and sperm met, you wouldn't be you. You would be someone else completely. Isn't that a mind-blowing thought?

Yet here you are. You made it here to earth at this time. None of this was an accident; it was all perfectly orchestrated to bring you here. You are a miracle. And I want you to start to believe that and live like you are. I want you to begin to live your cosmic purpose.

Furthermore, in case there was still any doubt about how magical you are, here's a little reminder that you are made of stardust. The atoms within you were made in a star. Many of them were formed at the beginning of the universe with the Big Bang, before the earth was even born. You've travelled through supernovas. There are elements within you from the same stars that also make up our earth and solar system. You are an intricate part of the universe connected to everything that has ever been and ever will be. You are the universe in a human body. You are made of bits of stars and cosmic dust. You are cosmic and therefore you have a cosmic purpose, which I hope this book will help you to uncover and begin to live.

As Thich Nhat Hanh beautifully said: 'The whole cosmos has come together to create you. You carry the whole cosmos inside you. That is why, to accept yourself and to love yourself is an expression of gratitude.'

This book will take you on a spiritual journey to discover more of your unique soul essence and to fully accept and love yourself. It will allow your soul and cosmic purpose to awaken and shine through you.

Spirituality is often defined as 'an individual's search for ultimate or sacred meaning, and purpose in life' and that's what this journey is – a journey towards finding meaning and purpose in your life and, in doing so, contributing and making a difference to the world and those around you in the way that only you can.

Because this is your cosmic purpose – to be YOU; to awaken the seeds of your soul, and your soul's dreams and desires, to bring what only you can bring and allow your soul to live through you.

Why It Is So Important That You Discover Your Purpose

Your purpose is not some elusive thing that lives outside of you that one day you may find and your whole life will suddenly change. Rather, your purpose is you – the you that you came here to be in this lifetime. Ultimately, if you don't discover this, you won't be living your most purposeful and authentic life.

How would your life change right now if you believed that to be true? That rather than your purpose being something outside of you that always just eludes you, your entire life is your purpose. The way you navigate difficulties, show up in the world, go to your job, share your wisdom, move through the world – it's all part of your purpose. Everything in your life has been chosen for you by your soul to help you grow into more of yourself and your purpose.

Your soul vibrates to a unique frequency that's needed in the world. The best way I can describe it is this: imagine listening to a beautiful choir singing, but there is no one singing soprano. Although it sounds ok, there is something missing that would make it even more wonderful and touch people in a more profound way. That's how the world feels when you don't allow yourself to vibrate at your unique soul frequency; like a little something is missing that could take the vibration of the world to the next level. We need your soul song, and this comes through you discovering and living your cosmic purpose.

What Happens When You Realise Your Purpose

When you begin to live a life of cosmic purpose, you start to trust in yourself and a greater guiding force weaving its way through your life. You trust that you are always being supported and that everything that happens in your life is an opportunity for you to learn, grow and evolve in some way. You allow your soul to live and experience life through you, and seek deeper wisdom and answers by going within rather than looking outside of you for anything. Most of all, you begin to understand that there is more to life than the mundane everyday existence that we're taught that life is all about. Instead, your life becomes spiritual, meaningful, purposeful and part of a divine plan.

People often ask me how to be spiritual and my answer is always the same – being spiritual isn't something you do; it's a way of life. I don't 'do spiritual things' and then get on with my life – spirituality *is* my life.

There is often a belief, especially in the beginning, that being spiritual means you should be incredibly serious and devout – so many stereotypes come into play. Indeed, there should be reverence towards your journey, but it doesn't need to become another way to beat yourself up. Life and the journey should be fun and enjoyable and lived to the full. So, notice if there is ever a little voice inside telling you, 'If you were spiritual, you wouldn't behave like that' or 'Spiritual people don't do that'.

What even is a 'spiritual person' anyway? Someone who wears all white and floats around barefoot, drinking green juice, chanting and never letting anything bother them? (Not that there is anything wrong with that if that's your soul's chosen path.) I'm just not sure that's real life for most people. I'm not sure that's how we truly live our cosmic purpose and share it with the world. It's so easy to be spiritual when you're floating around Bali with all the time in the world doing endless yoga classes and talking about the meaning of life all day. It's so easy to meditate when you're in a cave in the Himalayas with no one bothering you or pushing your buttons. But the real question is whether you can maintain that same sense of purpose, peace and connection to your soul in the 'real world' when there is traffic and noise and a job to go to and demands and people triggering you and expecting things from you. To me, true spirituality is being able to maintain presence and connection to the divine and who you truly are in these times. It is about making spirituality a way of life that helps you to navigate the world and all its wild, weird and wonderful ways so much more easily. That's true cosmic purpose – to bring the spiritual and divine into your everyday life.

Spirituality is an ongoing journey and one that never ends, as, when you have it all figured out, that's when you've completed soul school and leave the earth. So, my main piece of advice to you now as we begin this journey together towards more of your cosmic purpose is to enjoy the journey.

Don't rush it. Don't wish to know it all now. Allow the journey to unfold, just as it should.

‘Part of your cosmic purpose is to go beyond your ego and connect to your higher self and then your soul.’

Chapter 2

WHAT IS YOUR SOUL?

Let's dive a little deeper now into understanding more about the universe, your soul, your higher self and your ego so that we can start figuring out your exact cosmic purpose.

These concepts are interchangeable and go by many different names, and part of this comes from our human need to try to make sense of things and logically understand them and give them a name. But when we are talking about things of a cosmic and divine nature, they cannot be grasped by the human mind, only felt and experienced first hand, otherwise you are living someone else's interpretation and experience of the divine.

In this book, I will use the words 'universe', 'soul', 'higher self', 'cosmic consciousness' and 'ego' or 'human you', as those are what feel right for me. Each of these is described below with alternatives, so feel into what name, if any, feels best for you – this is your journey and your experience after all!

The universe

This is the source and essence of all existence. It's the infinite, eternal, expansive, wise, all-knowing energy that all life comes from, and all life will return to. It's the universal intelligence, the guiding life force energy, the higher power and consciousness that weaves through everything. This may also be called 'source', 'divine', 'consciousness', 'God' or 'Goddess', or any name that resonates most with you.

Your soul

Your soul is the unique expression of the universe contained within you which connects you to cosmic consciousness and the entire universe. If you imagine the universe as the ocean, your soul is a cup of water from that ocean. Your soul is formless and timeless – it has no beginning and no end; it is eternal. Our souls are pure energy and need to come to earth into this human body to experience this world and all that it is to be human. Your soul grows and evolves with each lifetime and carries the experiences of all your lifetimes. Your soul plants the seeds within you that it wants you to awaken in this lifetime and seeks learning, purpose, connection, growth, awakening, evolution, expansion and remembering through your human experience. Your soul may also be called 'spirit', 'soul self' or 'divine self'.

Your higher self

You may have also heard talk of your higher self. This is the most soulful, authentic, awakened version of you in this lifetime – the version of you who is connected to your soul and knows and understands the assignment. It's through uncovering, discovering and living as more of your higher self that you're able to remember and connect to the part of you who is eternal and divine, and begin to experience the essence of your soul, accessing more of your soul lessons and purpose. This may also be called your 'authentic self' or 'divine essence'.

Cosmic consciousness

When we talk of cosmic consciousness we are referring to the highest form of consciousness that comes from the universe. It is where all the wisdom, answers, direction, guidance and awareness of all that is, all that ever was, and all that will be exists. It's the realm of infinite possibilities, opportunities, perspectives, awareness and connection beyond the human mind. This may also be referred to as 'higher consciousness' or 'divine consciousness'.

Human you

Sometimes referred to as the ego, human you is often the biggest block to knowing your soul and trusting your cosmic purpose. It is the part of you who believes you to be separate from the universe and everyone and everything in it. Human you creates an identity based on your beliefs and experiences, and tries to protect and defend that identity from all perceived threats. It's the part of you who identifies with and attaches to the material world, status and achievements, and seeks approval, validation and answers from outside you.

It is your ego that causes you to identify not only with your physical body and what it looks like, but also every passing mood, thought, belief and feeling, believing this to be 'you' and who you are. It shapes how you perceive yourself and your image, identity, beliefs and self-worth. The ego is impulsive and reactive and driven by fear, control, attachment and separation, and sees most things in life as a threat to your existence.

When left unchecked and unobserved, your ego will run your life without you even knowing it and then you'll wonder why life is always difficult or why you feel so lost, disconnected, purposeless and empty. Part of your cosmic purpose is to go beyond your ego and human and societal conditioning and connect to your higher self and then your soul, and I hope to show you how in the pages of this book.

Now we've learned more about what your soul is, let's begin to look at the journey of your soul . . .

‘Every choice and decision you make and every action you take opens new directions and dimensions in your soul journey.’

Chapter 3

THE JOURNEY OF YOUR SOUL

I truly believe that, before we come to earth in each lifetime, we sit with our spirit guide and decide the lessons that we want to learn and what challenges, experiences and adventures we want to go through to evolve, transform and reach a new level of soul awakening and understanding. These may be based on things that need to be completed from past lifetimes or something entirely new that our soul wants to experience.

My belief is that we choose the exact moment when we will come to earth and the exact moment we will leave, and the circumstances around both. Our souls also choose our family, the conditions we will be born into, our gender and race; and, sometimes, these can be challenging, but it's in these challenges that we learn the most. We choose the challenges and difficulties we will go through to help us grow. We also call in those other souls who we need to work with through our life to learn the lessons that we need to. I truly believe that's why we sometimes find it so hard to let go of those people who really hurt us as, on a soul level, we knew and trusted them enough to cause us pain in this lifetime to help us learn what we need to learn.

We choose our cosmic purpose: what we are going to offer and share in this lifetime, how we can be of service and make a difference and shape the world in some way, and what soul dreams and desires are needed in the world right now that are going to be brought to life through us. We choose the themes that we want to experience and overcome in this lifetime. We choose who we want to be and how we want to learn to show up in the world.

And then we come to earth and forget it all.

That's part of the agreement: we forget so that, through the human journey, we can remember. Much of the spiritual journey isn't about learning anything; it's about forgetting what you've been taught that makes you doubt yourself and your power, magic and magnificence. It's about letting go of who and what you're not. It's a journey back home to your soul and remembering who you truly are and what you already know deep within you.

We also have free will as humans. Our soul may choose four or five big lessons for this lifetime, but how we move between or face these lessons, or whether we even do face any of it, is up to us once we come down to earth. We may give up after the first difficult thing that happens to us and stay stuck in patterns of victimhood, seeing life as hard or unfair and never recognising the challenges as lessons and opportunities for growth. Or we may never learn to trust and believe in ourselves and follow the nudges from our soul to bring certain things to life or go after what we truly desire, staying stuck in lack of self-worth and looking outside us for approval and answers.

We can make life as easy or as hard as we choose to as humans. Every choice and decision that you make and every action you take opens new directions and dimensions in your life and on your soul journey, which is why it's so important to try to make these consciously from the aspect of your soul self (rather than your ego) as this is what will take you closer towards your cosmic purpose and a life of meaning and spiritual connection. We'll explore simple ways to do this throughout this book.

I feel like we also forget because we have to. If we remembered how beautiful and easy and perfect life is as a soul, we'd want to go back home, to our soul life. In the moments when it gets too tough to be human, we'd simply wish to be back in our soul home where we exist in peace, love and bliss as pure consciousness. Because, as we all know, being a human isn't easy, and it's not meant to be! And neither is the spiritual journey. I feel as though there's a common misconception that, once we are on a spiritual journey, everything will become easier when, in fact, at times, the opposite can be true.

It is hard to take more personal responsibility for your own life and, especially at the beginning of my journey, I'd long for the days when I could blame others for how I was feeling or how my life was (or wasn't) working out. It can also be hard to accept the lessons and hardships that our souls sometimes need us to go through in order to evolve, learn and grow. I know there have been times in my own journey when I've felt frustration, confusion and even anger at my soul and my journey. But what I can promise you is that on the other side of any challenge is so much more understanding, bliss and connection.

Part of the reason our souls come here to earth is to experience the full spectrum of human emotions and experiences, and, as your soul evolves, you will likely choose more challenging lifetimes for yourself so that you can experience more of what it is to be a soul having a human experience. This is part of your cosmic purpose – to learn as much as you can through as many lifetimes and experiences as you can so that you can begin to share that wealth of your experience to guide others along their journey.

Each lifetime is an opportunity to remember that you are a soul having a human experience and to find your way back to your soul self, which we'll look at now . . .

‘The journey back to your soul is a remembering of who you truly are.’

Chapter 4

FINDING YOUR WAY BACK TO YOUR SOUL SELF

The spiritual journey back to your soul and towards living your cosmic purpose usually begins with a niggling dissatisfaction with life – a sense that there is more to you and life than you are currently experiencing, and a yearning for something more meaningful. The things that once brought you joy no longer seem to, especially the material things that you use to try to avoid feeling the dissatisfaction or to bring you a momentary high or quick fix – the shopping for new clothes, wild nights out, gossiping over a glass (or three!) of wine or the mindless scrolling and numbing.

This happened to me after Sharon's passing and the break-up of my relationship, which I spoke about in the Introduction. I worked in Marketing and PR and, as far as jobs went, it was a good job. But I'd get home at the end of every day and feel empty and purposeless, as though I hadn't made a difference at all in the world. The corporate world and all of its arbitrary rules made less and less sense to me as time went on and my soul began to speak louder. I knew it wasn't a world that I belonged in anymore.

You too may begin to dislike your job, relationship or current lifestyle without even being entirely sure why, but there is just a knowing within that it no longer gives you what you need. There is an emptiness, a void, perhaps a deep sadness or loneliness that you can't quite put your finger on, but a knowing that something in your life is not quite right. These initial stages of your awakening can feel confusing, unsettling and incredibly lonely. You may wish that you could go back to your 'old life', but there is no going back once your soul begins to stir and calls you back home to yourself.

The more you try to resist, the harder it all seems to get; the more you try to hide, the more problems will find you; the more you try to lose yourself in your old ways and old life, the more empty you will feel; the more you try to ignore the niggles, the louder they will call, as your soul tries to find ways to awaken you and bring you back on to your path and into your unique soul frequency.

Your soul is always trying to speak to you and call you into more of your higher self and purpose. Every time you feel a niggle of discontent or a deep knowing that there is something more to you and life, you are being called forward into a new timeline, a new version of you and your life. This is a powerful moment, and the more you can begin to consciously listen to and follow the whispers from your soul, the more meaningful, soul-led and blissful your life will begin to become.

That's not to say that the spiritual journey is easy; it isn't. It's one of the hardest paths to take, and that's why so few take it and instead spend their whole lives moaning about how awful or difficult life is, or how they wish they could be happier, or if only this or that thing would change, things would be ok.

So, I honour you for listening to the whispers from your soul and picking up this book at all. It takes huge courage. Although this journey may be challenging at times, I promise you it is so incredibly worth it.

The journey back to your soul is a remembering of who you truly are and, to help with that, I'd love you to do something for me. Point at yourself, right now. I mean it. Point at yourself. Where did you point to? I'm going to take a pretty good guess that it wasn't your head but somewhere around your heart. Doesn't this just show more about the truth of who you really are? You are not your thoughts or doubts or the noise that's in your head all the time. You are something way more that lives within your heart. It is said that your heart is the place through which your soul speaks, hoping you will hear.

There is so much more to you than what you have been led to believe, and I want to reintroduce you to that part of you in the pages of this book. Through the journey back to your soul, you uncover all the parts of you that you have hidden, reclaim all the parts of you that you have abandoned, find all the parts of you that you have lost and remember all the parts of you that are divine and connected to the whole universe.

You begin to uncover your gifts and talents and share them. You start to be of service to the world in the way that only you can, awakening all the dreams and desires that are needed in the world and can only be brought to life through you. You step fully back on to the path of your soul, moving and weaving through this lifetime as your soul intended you to.

Through struggles you find your strength; through darkness you find your light; through fear you find your faith; through despair you find your hope and through it all you find yourself – a deep remembering that you are a cosmic soul and came here with a cosmic purpose.

The initial stages of the journey will likely have you looking for answers. You may come to books like this or feel a calling to explore certain healing methods or a deep desire to know more about the spiritual world and, as this whole new world opens up for you, it can feel confusing and overwhelming. You have one person telling you that this is the right way and another person telling you that that is the right way, and so many experts and options and things to explore. There are so many pathways back to your soul – from time in nature to crystals, astrology, meditation, spiritual studies and thousands of different books and teachers. But the greatest teacher by far is you and your own journey, and one of the greatest gifts I hope you gain from this book is to become your own teacher and find your own truth through first-hand personal experience.

I want you to take your time as you begin this journey, allow it to unfold and enjoy the ride. So often we want to rush and have all the answers now, but very often things will only reveal themselves as we are ready, as the famous saying goes, 'when the student is ready the teacher will appear'.

I often look back to the beginning of my journey with such fondness for the starry-eyed, eager, keen version of me back then. As much as she felt lost, confused and frustrated most of the time, those initial years of growth and exploration were tender and beautiful, and filled with such awe, wonder and discoveries, which created the foundations that the rest of my journey was built upon.

This journey can also feel lonely. You may feel that you are the only one walking this path and, as you begin to change and grow and evolve, there will be a natural separation from who you once were, the life you once lived and what you once believed to be true. It can feel like you suddenly have nothing in common with those around you and no desire to continue to do certain things or live the way that you used to.

People will fall away as you walk this path – it's a sad yet inevitable truth, and you need to allow them to leave with love. As you uncover more of who you are and make changes in your life, this will bother those who have always known you as a certain version of you or benefited from you behaving in a certain way. There will be push back and resistance and even perhaps ridicule or confusion or fear from those around you who want you to remain the same. But we are not meant to remain the same. We are here to grow and evolve and experience many different versions of ourselves on our journey back to our true soul self. I also promise you that you doing this work will inspire so many others around you to begin to explore the same for themselves.

The initial part of your journey begins with uncovering and letting go of all that keeps you from truly knowing who you are. You need to take radical responsibility for your own life and journey, and that's why the journey can be challenging to begin with as it's way 'easier' to keep allowing it to be someone or something else's fault that your life is the way it is. But it's through this part of the journey that you will really begin to know, trust, understand and believe in yourself like never before.

There will be times on this journey when life makes absolutely no sense anymore and you no longer feel like you belong. But it's in these moments when you lose parts of yourself that you truly find yourself. This journey will be one of the hardest, most challenging yet utterly magical, life-changing, fulfilling and meaningful journeys that you will ever take, and I promise you that, in one of the first moments you touch the divine or have a deep soul remembering or step into your soul power, it will be so, so worth it.

Through this journey you will not only remember who you are and what you came here for, but you'll begin to uncover what makes you authentically you and start to live life in flow with the universe and your soul, even in the more challenging times. When you begin to live your life as a soul having a human experience, you begin to see earth as soul school, somewhere you've come to learn, and that's when life gets magical. You suffer the most in life when you believe yourself separate from your soul and the universe; I want to help you to find your way back.

WAYS TO UNCOVER YOUR COSMIC PURPOSE

We now enter Part 2 of this journey where you get to explore more of your cosmic purpose and the many ways to live it, but, first, there is something I want to share with you.

As we explore concepts such as spirit guides, past lives and soul contracts in the chapters that follow, I would love for you to go into this with an open and curious mind. Try not to have any preconceived ideas or expectations as to how you think it should be or how these things will make themselves known to you. These all come from your ego mind that just loves to prove all of this wrong as it doesn't want you moving beyond its grip into higher levels of consciousness and awareness that it just can't grasp and understand. That is why your ego will work so hard to make you doubt that any of this is true and have you constantly second-guessing yourself. This is where, yet again, you are called into trusting your soul and practising patience along this journey.

Before we begin, I want to talk to you about spiritual protection and how to create your space as this is vitally important when you begin to explore other realms.

The Importance of Creating Sacred Space

Creating your space just means being in a safe and sacred space to do this work. You all know by now that I am a huge fan of altars and I create one wherever I go. This is where I go to do my daily spiritual devotion. An altar can be as simple as a small space in your home with crystals and incense, but you can add anything to your altar that you like, such as candles, images or statues. My travelling altar usually has crystals, incense and a candle, and I also gather something from the earth wherever I am.

Personally, I like to energetically clear the space before I begin by burning Palo Santo (or you can use sage or incense). I also clear my energy with Florida water (or you can use aura sprays or essential oils). You might like to play gentle relaxing music and have some incense burning.

The Art of Grounding Yourself and Protecting Your Energy

Before beginning any work with guides or where you will be going to other realms, you must ground and protect your energy. To ground, take some really long, slow, deep breaths and connect yourself to the support and safety of the earth beneath you. You might want to visualise roots moving from you deep into the earth, anchoring and connecting you to the earth's energy.

To protect your energy, visualise a shield or protective bubble surrounding you. You may visualise this bubble as bright white radiant light, or any other colour that resonates most with you. Feel its impenetrable protection surround you, knowing that you are safe.

As you come to know your spirit guide and/or guardian angel, archangels and ascended masters as the chapters unfold, call on them to be with you and protect you. Begin your practices with a prayer for protection and guidance, such as 'Please protect and guide me and allow only that which is love, light and truth.'

CRYSTAL SUGGESTIONS TO ENHANCE YOUR JOURNEY

If you want to work with crystals in your practices, here are some of the best for protection, and also connecting to your soul:

- **Black tourmaline:** one of the most protective crystals, black tourmaline will form a protective shield around you and help you to stay grounded.

- **Amethyst:** known as a spiritual protector, amethyst also helps you to connect to higher levels of consciousness and awakens your psychic abilities.
- **Selenite:** this will help to clear and protect the energy of your space and connect you to your soul's purpose, seeking higher guidance and wisdom.
- **Amazez:** a journeying crystal, amazez will help you to connect to your inner world and soul self, and trust and follow your intuition.
- **Super seven:** this helps you to unlock ancient wisdom and invites you to explore deeper connections to higher frequencies, the divine consciousness and the spiritual realm.

(Crystals and other products, such as candles and Palo Santo, that you might like to use on your altar can be purchased from https://www.soulemporium.com.)

As you journey through Part 2, don't forget to reflect, journal and meditate on the 'whispers from your soul'.

‘You get to choose, in each unfolding moment in the story of your life, who you want to be and how you want to show up in the world.’

Chapter 5

YOU MUST REALISE WHO YOU'RE NOT

Much of this journey begins with forgetting who you're not, to remember who you are.

One of the things that causes you the most pain and suffering in life is when you are supressing your soul's unique expression and not living the life that you are meant to – spending all of your time and energy trying to morph yourself into someone you're not; behaving in the way you think others want you to behave; staying stuck in situations, patterns, behaviours and relationships that don't serve you; trying to hide and shrink parts of yourself; and seeking approval, validation and permission from the outside world.

This is when your life feels the most sad, low and purposeless, and you feel unhappy as you cut yourself off from the very source of your power. You deny your own cosmic purpose – the very reason you came here to earth, which is to be you and allow your unique essence to flow through you. There are words your soul wants to speak through you, things it wants to create through you, lessons it wants to be learned through you, magic it wants to weave through you, boundaries it wants to be set through you and experiences it wants to have through you. The whole time you're trying to pretend to be someone you're not, your soul cannot live its essence through you.

The reason that you forgot who you are – a soul having a human experience with a cosmic purpose on earth – is not entirely your fault. We live in a world that disconnects you from your true source of power. A consumerist world that profits from you never feeling like you're enough and that you need something outside of you to feel happy and fulfilled. A noisy, overstimulating world that profits from your awareness, attention and time, and will pull you in every direction outside of yourself to look at this or that shiny thing. A world of social media where you are comparing your real life to somebody else's curated highlight reel.

We're told that we need status, cars, houses, titles and a wealth of other things to make us happy, and so we look for our purpose outside of us in these things. But eventually this ends up feeling empty and unfulfilling, and that's because none of this is who you truly are. You will never find your true purpose and meaning in something that you're not.

I want you to remember that you are not your job title, relationship status, where you live, what you drive, your social circle, your looks or your body. You are not your habits, patterns and beliefs that keep you doubting yourself, your worth and your part to play in the world. You are not your past or your mistakes or what has happened in your life. You're not even who you were yesterday.

You get to choose, in each unfolding moment in the story of your life, who you want to be and how you want to show up in the world, and therefore begin to live out your cosmic purpose.

Forgetting Who You're Not

Begin this process by getting honest about those places in your life where you're afraid to be all of you. Perhaps you act one way with one group and another way with another. Of course, there are going to be times when perhaps the professional work version of you is a little different to the home version of you. But begin to get honest about where you are really morphing yourself and trying to pretend to be someone you're not to fit in with the people you're with or the situations you're in, and why.

As you do this, you're going to be able to see where you have shrunk, hidden and dimmed parts of yourself and given away your inner authority, letting others or the outside world affect how you feel, what you do and who you can be.

You'll begin to see the parts of you that aren't truly you and keep you out of alignment with your soul self. Those doubts, fears and limiting beliefs that tell you you're not enough or tell you to act this way or speak that way, where do they even come from? Usually, it's something that has been given to you from the outside world, well-meaning caregivers, advertising or social media.

You are also not your past or all that has happened to you in the past. Imagine that I clicked my fingers right now and erased your entire past. That's right, everything that has happened in your life before this moment has gone, your entire history. Who would you be? Right now, in this moment, who would you be without all that has happened in your past?

So very often we allow ourselves to be defined by the past believing that we are the way we are because of what has happened to us. We allow past experiences to mould and shape us, and we continue to perpetuate the same cycles and patterns by behaving in the same way or believing the same things over and over again and thinking that this is who we are.

You are not the stories that you tell yourself about you and your life. Giving up the stories of your past is one of the most empowering parts of this journey. Yes, all that has happened to you has brought you here, to this moment, and it's important to learn from the past. But while you continue to tell yourself that you or your life are the way they are because of what happened to you in a long-gone past, you can't become who you're here to be. You cannot get to your future while your past is still present.

Did you know that our memories are not even that accurate? Research has shown that we can alter our memories, adding and removing certain parts and remembering them differently each time we tell them.[1] Our memories are stories that we tell about our past, not necessarily 100 per cent fact.

You are also not the stories that your ego tells you; the stories about how you're too much or not enough. The stories about what you are and aren't capable of, or what you can and cannot do, or what you have or haven't achieved. The more you repeat your stories to yourself and others, the more they become your reality, but this does not mean that they are true or define who you are.

Neither are you the versions of you who exist in other people's minds or who they want you to be. There are thousands and thousands of versions of you who exist in other people's minds and none of these is who you truly are. You are not the beliefs that others have put upon you or their expectations or the versions of you who they want you to be to fit their own narratives about who you are, life and the way it should be.

You aren't your pain or your wounding, your shame or your fears or your worries. You aren't the parts of you that are scared and stuck and afraid. You are not your beliefs, thoughts or behaviours, and you can change all of these in any moment, which we'll explore in later chapters.

The journey towards your cosmic purpose begins with forgetting who you're not and letting go of the parts of you and your life that keep you out of vibrational alignment with your soul. It's about going inwards and working on removing all the obstacles to knowing your true self and healing all those things that keep you out of alignment with your unique soul's vibration.

If you're ready to remember who you are before the world told you who to be, let's continue by healing your worth wound so that you can begin to radiate more of your soul's essence.

WHISPERS FROM YOUR SOUL

- Can you identify who you are not? Look at your life story and what that is – is it a story about not being good enough, never being chosen, that you're too shy or stupid to do x or y, or that things never work out for you?
- Start to catch yourself in that story and begin to tell yourself a new one – that you are always being supported and guided, that you have a reason for being here and that you have so much to offer just by being you.
- Having read all of this, who do you want to be and how do you want to show up in the world?

‘Every part of you is exactly as your soul intended it to be in this lifetime.’

Chapter 6

HEAL YOUR WORTH WOUND

One of the greatest ways that you can begin to live your cosmic purpose is to heal your worth wound – that deep-rooted belief that you are less than, that constant feeling of never being enough and, ultimately, that profound sense of being unworthy. You can never fully be all of who your soul came here to be if you are worried that you are not good enough or about the shape of your thighs or a wrinkle on your forehead. This is yet another way that the current systems keep you disconnected from the power of your divinity – by making you feel like you are never enough.

When you identify too much with human you and your looks, material possessions and gaining approval and validation from the world outside of you, you disconnect from the beauty, power, essence, magnificence and magic of your soul. When you walk through the world not feeling like you are enough, you suffocate the life force energy of your soul.

This isn't to say that you don't need to make the best of yourself or take care of yourself – your human body is the vessel for your soul, so you want to take the best care of it possible and feel as good in it as you can so that your soul can live, experience and express fully through you. Get enough sleep, eat well, hydrate, exercise and learn how to breathe properly, meditate, walk in nature and keep your energy clear so that your soul essence can flow through you. Yes, your soul made you perfectly, but you can't abuse and not take care of your human vessel and expect life force energy to be able to flow through it clearly.

The problem comes when you are doing things because you feel that you *need* to do them to fit in or be accepted, because you feel you *should* look a certain way or because you don't feel good enough without it. I need you to remember that there is an entire industry that profits from you never feeling like you're enough.

One of the most powerful ways to take someone's power is to make them dislike themselves. And we live in a world that's designed to make you feel like you're not enough just as you are. This has you constantly chasing things outside of you and feeling like you need something out there to make you feel worthy or that you need to look or behave a certain way to be enough. I want you to come to see that it's all already within you. When you begin to take back your worth and realise who you truly are, your life will change. Your soul created you just the way you are for a reason – you are perfect in your soul's eyes, and I wish that each one of you could see yourself through the eyes of your soul, or even what I see when I look at you.

I see your soul shining through, your inner beauty radiating outwards, your unique expression of the universe in a human body and everything that makes you YOU. You are radiant and magical and perfect just as you are. Every part of you is exactly as your soul intended it to be in this lifetime.

But we can only see you when you allow your soul to express and radiate out of you, when you stop squishing your soul's essence by worrying too much about whether you look the way the latest beauty standard tells you that you should look or you're behaving the way you should be behaving. In order to fully live your cosmic purpose and allow your soul to radiate and experience life through you, you need to heal your wounds around your sense of self and not feeling like enough.

Undoing Your Worth Wounds

Let's begin by reflecting on where your worth wounds have come from:

- What has happened in your life that has made you feel like you're not enough?
- Who or what has made you doubt yourself and question your worth?
- Where does the belief come from that you're not worthy?
- What are the stories that you tell yourself about who you are and what you do or don't deserve?
- What has made you forget your divine cosmic essence and who you truly are?

In order to expand into your full soul self, you need to let go of all that keeps you from being able to fully love, accept and approve of yourself. Do healing around any ways in which you've felt different, an outsider or not believed in yourself, your gifts and what you have to offer to the world. Hold those versions of you who felt this way and let them know that you accept and love all parts of you and that it is safe to be all of who you are.

It's time to realise that you are enough just as you are and that everything that makes you YOU is needed in the world. It's time to embrace your quirks, uniqueness and everything about you that makes you different, and see this as a superpower rather than a flaw. You are perfect just the way you are and, when you begin to embrace your unique soul essence and let your soul's light shine through you, that's when you will radiate your true worth.

Because, my love, as you begin to allow your soul to weave and express through you and listen once more to the stirrings of your heart and soul, you will begin to know yourself, understand yourself, accept yourself, value yourself and love yourself once more.

And, as you do this, you will no longer accept anything less than you deserve. You will begin to know that you are worthy and deserving and more than enough just as you are. From here, you will begin to trust yourself and believe in yourself enough to listen to your intuition and inner knowing, and follow where your soul wants you to go. You will be empowered to care for, nurture, nourish and look after yourself as the cosmic being that you are.

It's only from a place of being fully anchored, grounded and at home in yourself and your values, worth and sense of self that you will ever be able to truly make change, move forwards and do things differently in your life. This is the only place from which you can truly know what you want and then believe in yourself enough to get it.

What the world really needs is you being all of you; that's a huge part of your cosmic purpose – to bring you to the world, which you can't do when you don't feel worthy or good enough. To do this, you need to once more connect back to the essence of your soul, as it's only when you are disconnected from the divine and living too much from your ego that you will feel like you're not enough.

The way to create a life of meaning and purpose is to know yourself, love yourself and accept yourself as the soul that you are. All of you – the complex, raw, vulnerable, messy, perfectly imperfect human you, alongside the powerful, wise, magical, all-knowing soul you. As soon as you can begin to show up in the world as who you truly are without questioning it, that's when you become free.

When you are truly rooted, anchored and grounded into your

sense of self, you no longer need to look for as much from the outside world. You self-source your worth, approval, validation and permission from within you, and that's when real change and transformation becomes possible. You begin to know from deep within you what you are worthy, deserving and capable of.

I'd love you to begin to feel into who you are when you are at your very best and most purposeful – when you are your truest, most authentic soul self. What makes you feel good, alive, like your best, most soulful self? Let more of this version of you begin to shine through. And then start to embody that energy.

You see, it's not enough to just tell yourself that you're worth more or that you'll believe in yourself more, as, very often, especially in times of difficulty or doubt, your ego mind will simply tell you, 'No you aren't' or 'No you won't'. You can tell yourself something until you're blue in the face and it won't make too much difference until you begin to *feel* and embody it; that's where the true wisdom and awareness – gnosis – lies. It doesn't come from the mind; it comes from the body. The more you can embody deep levels of worth, power, confidence and value and know who you are deep in your bones, the more you'll begin to embody your soul and your new beliefs, and the more your life will change.

When you feel a sense of worth from deep within you and a sense of trust deep in your soul, that's when you're going to truly show up in the world differently. You simply won't accept anything less than you deserve. When you accept and love yourself for all of who you are, you won't be available for anything or anyone that doesn't reflect that – these things just won't come into your consciousness anymore. Every now and then, they may show up to give you a little test of whether you're holding that energetic boundary and knowing what you deserve, but, for the most part, those things will stay away from you.

I finally want to mention that many people come to the spiritual journey from a place of not feeling good enough. When you approach your spiritual journey or anything in life from a place of lack and doing it because you're not good enough or need 'fixing' or because you feel worthless in some way, it's going to feel hopeless, like hard work and as though you're always searching for that one elusive thing that will make you feel complete.

You need to approach this journey from a place of empowerment and finding your way back to your soul and more of your authentic soul self, not because there is anything wrong with you or missing. All that is truly missing is your connection to the essence and truth of who you are and, once you find that, you'll realise that you are inherently worthy just because you are alive. There never was and never will be anything wrong with you – you just got a little lost along the way and forgot the magnificence of your soul.

Now that you have started to heal your worth wounds and realise that you are more than enough just as you are, let's move to the mind and remember that you are not your thoughts . . .

WHISPERS FROM YOUR SOUL

- Where do you currently derive most of your sense of self-worth?
- Who or what makes you doubt and question yourself the most and why?
- Who are you at your most purposeful, soulful, wild and free self?

‘Allow your soul self to emerge from behind the thoughts.’

Chapter 7

REMEMBER, YOU ARE NOT YOUR THOUGHTS

One thing that will keep you from ever truly living a life of cosmic purpose is identifying with your thoughts and believing that they are who you are. Your thoughts operate from your ego, from fear. Your thoughts are the part of you that keeps you separate from higher consciousness and universal wisdom, and from knowing yourself as a soul and part of the divine.

Your thoughts will try to trick you and 'keep you safe' and have you doubting your intuition, inner knowing and soul self. Unless you become aware of it, your mind will run a constant commentary on your life, churning out words, judgements, stories, opinions, memories and predictions all day long.

In fact, do something for me now: close your eyes for the next 30 seconds or so and just observe your mind. Notice where it goes, what it says, what its latest story is or what today's worries are. Try not to get attached to any of your thoughts, just watch them; be the observer.

The very fact that you were just able to observe your thoughts shows that you are not your thoughts – they are simply experiences that you are having in this moment that, over time, you have identified with and believed to be who you are. But you are so much more than your thoughts and, once you begin to realise this, your life will start to change in so many beautiful ways.

Think of it like this: take any object right now – a stone, crystal or pen – and run it across the palm of your hand. Your hand is you, the object is your thoughts, feelings and emotions that run through you, but they are not you. Now, grip the object. This is what happens when you identify with your thoughts and believe them to be you, holding on to them. Notice too how it feels to grip and hold – there is tension and struggle, and it feels like hard work. At any time, you can let go of that object – it's not you. You can do the same with your thoughts.

Another way to put it is this: imagine if I asked you to listen to the sounds around you now or observe what you can see in the space you're currently in. You'd all agree that what you can hear and see are separate from you and you are the one doing the seeing and hearing. You are also the one watching your thoughts, yet why do we find it so hard to separate ourselves from our thoughts and be able to see ourselves as the one who observes these thoughts rather than the thoughts themselves?

We suffer because we believe our thoughts to be true, to be who we are. We personalise them and allow our thoughts to take over our whole lives and keep us in loops and spirals of uncertainty, doubt and questions without answers. We live in a world that prides logic, solutions and thinking over inner knowing, intuition and inner nudges. We think instead of feel. We try to justify and rationalise our soul whispers and make them make sense, which they very rarely do to the mind as it operates from fear and separation and doesn't understand the higher levels of divine consciousness that our soul operates from.

Don't get me wrong, our minds are brilliant tools when used

in the right way and they can help us to act, organise and solve a problem. The mind can take you to huge levels of success in life and helps to define your view of you and the world around you. The problems occur when your thoughts aren't supportive and are fear-based, keeping you captive in a small, ego-led life. Think of how many times in your life you have imagined fake scenarios and made up stories in your mind that aren't even true and hurt yourself or held yourself back as a result.

All of your thoughts are either worries about a long-gone past that cannot be changed or an imagined future that isn't even here yet. This keeps you out of the present, which is the only place your soul exists. You miss your entire life while you are trapped in your head listening to its stories.

Becoming Aware of Your Thoughts

As soon as you begin to observe your thoughts, you are no longer a slave to them and can instead begin to become the observer of your mind's current experience while you sink deeper into your soul. You get to become the universal awareness, the observer, your soul self and watch the screenplay of your mind.

As you begin to notice, watch and listen to your thoughts and realise that you are not your thoughts, you get to begin to question them. One thing I often like to ask in moments when my mind is catastrophising and jumping to the worst possible outcome or viewing a situation as much worse than it is, is 'Is that true?' That one question immediately helps me to separate from the thought and begin to question it and start to look at the same issue through the lens of my soul.

It is said that 95 per cent of our thoughts are unconscious, which keeps us stuck in the same loops, patterns, behaviours, habits and emotions. So many of our decisions and actions are made subconsciously without us even realising it. Your thoughts influence your emotions, which influence your actions and behaviours, which influence the outcome.

Becoming aware of your thoughts means that you can catch your limiting thoughts in the moments when they arise and replace them with ones that are more positive, visualising the outcome you want and reprogramming your mind. So, if you notice your mind telling you all the ways that something won't work out, think about one way that it possibly could. Each time you find yourself having a negative thought, flip it to something more positive – 'I can't do anything right' flips to 'I'm trying my best'; 'I'm not where I want to be in life' flips to 'I am taking steps towards where I want to go and know that I will get there'; or 'It's all my fault' flips to 'I did the best with what I knew at the time and, now I know better, I can do better'. You can also try removing the word 'should' from your vocabulary and replacing it with 'could'. Telling yourself what you *should* do often comes from a place of shame, blame or failure, whereas *could* gives you a choice and new possibilities.

Doing these things helps you to begin to make more conscious decisions and choices for yourself, your future and your life. Your greatest fears and biggest dreams are both just thoughts in your mind, and your life is shaped by which one you most choose to listen to.

Notice too how many times you say, 'I AM anxious' or 'I AM stressed' – no YOU are not anxious or stressed, that is not who you are. You *feel* anxious or stressed. Change your language around that and you'll immediately begin to separate yourself from what you are thinking and feeling, and become the observer, aligning more with your soul.

Meditation can also allow you to observe your thoughts from the seat of your soul. There is a common misconception with meditation that we are trying to stop our thoughts. We're not. If you stopped thinking, you wouldn't be alive. Instead, we are trying to distance you from your thoughts. So, a thought can come into your mind and, rather than attach to it, follow it and become it, you simply get to observe it and allow it to pass through. Start to practise this on a regular basis, either setting a timer for five minutes and simply observing your mind or setting various timers throughout the day and, when they go off, noticing where your mind is and what you are thinking about. You'll honestly amaze yourself by where your mind wanders!

In times when you are having a difficult or anxious moment or finding yourself in a hard situation or feeling sad or troubled, pause and notice what you are thinking. It is nearly always your thoughts or stories about the situation that are causing you the most upset. Remember that you are not your thoughts – it's only a thought and a thought can be changed. Become the awareness behind your thoughts – allow your soul self to emerge from behind the thoughts and be in the present moment; the only moment that ever really exists.

Let's move from our thoughts now into one of the more challenging yet transformative experiences you may encounter on your spiritual journey – the dark night of the soul.

WHISPERS FROM YOUR SOUL

- ❍ Does your mind tend to worry most about the past or the future?
- ❍ How often do you make up stories in your mind that aren't even true and hurt yourself or hold yourself back?
- ❍ What are your most repetitive thoughts and how can you now start to flip these?

‘In the darkness,
you are growing into
something way more
beautiful.’

Chapter 8

UNDERSTAND THE DARK NIGHT OF THE SOUL

One of the things that draws many people to a spiritual journey or wanting to discover more of their cosmic purpose is what is commonly called a 'dark night of the soul'. This could be initiated by illness, a shock relationship break-up or loss, death or something else that comes in and shakes the very foundations of your life.

It may be a dark night experience that starts you on your spiritual journey looking for answers or it may be that it happens when you feel as though you are already on a spiritual path. This can be confusing as it suddenly feels like life has turned against you, but, rest assured, it's a common occurrence in the early stages of a spiritual journey as you begin to awaken within you what has been dormant for so long – both the light and the shadows. In truth, though, a dark night of the soul can happen at any time through your journey when your soul needs to get your attention and take you into a new level of consciousness and evolution.

A dark night of the soul isn't just one night, as it sounds, but any difficult, challenging or painful time in your life when you feel utterly lost, hopeless, empty and disconnected. During a dark night, life seems to lose all purpose and meaning, and you lose hope and your faith. Nothing makes sense anymore; and you begin to question what your entire life is about. It can feel like nothing is working and even that life is against you.

Although it feels challenging and difficult, this is a time of huge transition and rebirth into something new, and a time of real spiritual awakening and evolution. It helps us to face who we thought we were and what we thought life was all about. It allows what is no longer in resonance to crumble so that a new higher version of us can appear. The dark night comes to shake us awake from where we've been sleepwalking through life.

During this process, hidden parts of us come up that need to be released. For example, the sadness or loneliness you've avoided fully feeling, which has kept your heart from opening up again to love or the sense of powerlessness that has come from all the times you gave yourself away or allowed someone else to decide the direction of your life. It may feel like it's coming all at once and, in a way, it is, but it's coming up to show you what is keeping you out of the vibration of your soul and stuck in your ego and human you.

It's important to think of these dark nights as quantum leaps in life. Your soul knows all that you are capable of and wants to jump you forward into a new timeline, but your ego wants to resist and remain, so there is a moment of struggle where parts of your ego must die for you to be able to evolve into something new. These times in life feel so sombre and challenging as a part of you dies; a set of beliefs, limiting thoughts, an old identity, a toxic behaviour – whatever it may be, something within you dies.

I've been through a few dark nights of the soul, and each time I can truthfully say that a huge shift and evolution has followed each one. My life has never been the same again. The first one is usually the most challenging as you have no idea what is going on or how to navigate it, and mine came quite early in my spiritual journey, not long after Sharon's passing. I was immersed in my spiritual practices, feeling a deep connection to myself, the divine and my soul's path, when the darkness unexpectedly took hold. I remember feeling so homesick during this time, but for my spiritual 'home'. It felt like life made absolutely no sense anymore and I no longer wanted to be part of this world. This was in no way in a dark sense, but, rather, through the spiritual work I had been doing, I encountered the bliss of my soul for the first time, which made human existence seem so bleak.

My first dark night seemed to last the longest. I had one foot in the spiritual world and one foot in the mundane world I'd lived in for so long. My old world no longer made any sense, but my new world hadn't opened up yet. I was no longer who I was, but I wasn't yet who I was becoming. A part of me had died, but the new me hadn't yet been born. This is the same for each dark night of the soul – the dark night is the place in between, the void, the wilderness, the rock bottom, the point of no return.

Embracing the Dark Nights

It may help to think of this in the same way as the journey between a caterpillar and a butterfly. The caterpillar is living caterpillar life, thinking that this is the way that life is and it's as good as it gets. Then something stirs from within, an inner calling you might say, that there is more to life – why crawl when you can fly? And so, the caterpillar goes within and turns into mush. It is no longer a caterpillar, not yet a butterfly and, instead, it is mush, dissolving away parts of itself it no longer needs. You may look at this part of the process and think this was the end, that it was over and yet . . .

Within that mush is also everything needed to grow into a butterfly and, over the course of the next few weeks, a transformation – a complete metamorphosis – happens and out of that mush and darkness emerges the most beautiful butterfly ready to take flight into the next part of its journey.

In a dark night of the soul, you are in the mush. And as much as you may look at the mush and think there is no way anything beautiful can come from this, the same is true of your dark night – in the darkness, you are growing into something way more beautiful. You are undergoing a transformation, with parts of you breaking down and dissolving and parts of you awakening and growing.

The more you can surrender to this process and think of it as a chrysalis of transformation, the more you can embrace the dark nights of the soul as a necessary part of your spiritual awakening and evolution. Because on the other side of a dark night of the soul your life will never be the same again. Everything changes – who you were, what was important to you, what matters to you, the way you see the world; everything changes. It's only when you've been in the depths of the darkness that you get to fully appreciate, embody and embrace the light when you get to the other side.

It's also important to remember that, when you are in the dark night, there is nothing wrong with you that needs fixing. Don't try to struggle with what you are experiencing or make it wrong or try to 'high vibe' your way out of it. I think that one of the biggest disservices we have created in the modern-day manifesting world is the fear that if you have one bad day or week, you're going to ruin your whole life.

I agree that we don't want to stay in low vibes or downward spirals for long periods of time, which we will look at later in this book. But neither do we want to bypass huge spiritual transformation by trying to deny how we're feeling or rushing the process.

Instead, allow yourself to go through this deep process of transformation. Remember that this too shall pass. Hold yourself gently. Turn towards yourself and what you are feeling rather than away from it. Go into the darkness and let it speak to you.

Embrace it rather than resist it. Look at what is coming up for you. Be honest about how you're feeling and feel your feelings. Explore where these feelings are coming from and what they are showing you. Use this as an opportunity to allow parts of you to die away, especially the parts that are in most resistance – let them go, with love.

Not only will all of this take you closer to your soul, but it will also help you to trust yourself, to know that you are not going anywhere and will be there for you even in your deepest and darkest times. This is when you truly begin to create such deep levels of self-trust, which, in turn, help you to access your higher self and your soul.

It's in these moments when you feel like you are losing your faith that you find it. It's so easy to trust in you and the universe and life when you're skipping down the street and the sun is shining and the birds are singing. If you can find your faith when your whole life is crumbling and falling apart, that's when it is real. That is faith that has been forged in the fires of despair.

If you can trust when you can see no way out or no way it's going to get better or when there is no meaning, that is true faith and that is the faith that will drive you to greater meaning and purpose because you will trust in yourself and the universe like never before, having gone through a dark night of the soul.

A Word from Me . . .

The irony is not lost on me that, during the writing of this book in summer 2024, I went through one of the deepest dark nights of the souls I have been through in a long time. Having to write about how your soul has a purpose and to trust in the unfolding of your life at a time when your faith is being tested, you seem to have lost the spiritual spark and you don't feel as though you have anything to offer to the world is a true initiation.

But that's exactly the point of these times – they are an initiation into something deeper, something greater. They pull you into deeper levels of faith and trust, and ask you to meet parts of yourself that you have been hiding from and face fears that have been causing you to remain small.

I tried to fight this dark night; trust me I did. And all that happened is that it got darker. It was only when I stopped, surrendered and looked deeply within that it all started to make more sense.

First of all, my faith was being tested. Did I really believe in all that I was writing? In moments of darkness and emptiness, could I really lean into trust and surrender, and believe that this was happening for my own highest good and to teach me something? Could I really believe that this was part of my soul's plan and that this was all taking me towards something even more wonderful?

Second, my ego was afraid of the deep responsibility of writing a book like this and putting myself out there and being seen as a spiritual teacher, and it was trying to keep me 'safe' by bringing up all the old fears around not being worthy. Even though I have walked this path for decades, I was now being asked to lay out the beliefs I live by and dive deeper into subjects I've only briefly discussed publicly before.

We struggle to be able to help or empathise with others unless we have been where they are. We can sympathise and try to support, but it's only when we have truly been where someone else is that we can fully understand and offer full support from a place of embodied wisdom. This is why everything that we experience in life is taking us towards more of our cosmic purpose, even the most difficult and challenging times. It's likely the times when you are going through a dark night of the soul that are forging you into a version of you who will be able to help others going through the same thing in the future.

Which is what I realised with this dark night. I now get to share my words, beliefs and wisdom with you from a place of it truly being tested and coming through that test. I understand how it feels for those of you coming to this work, hearing these things for the first time and not being totally sure if you believe them or can see a time when you will be able to fully live by them and trust your soul. I get to share with you just how I worked through and processed this time, and the breakthroughs that came on the other side of it.

Everything that I ever share with you comes from a place of first-hand experience and embodiment of walking the path. I can only ever share with you what I have been through myself. And so, I realised that this dark night, as hard as it felt, was, as always, in perfect timing. My soul had a plan and all I needed to do was dive deep into the initiation that I was being offered.

Was I going to let the 'not enough' and fear stop me from moving to this next level of my evolution and offering? Or was I going to hold the afraid parts of me and allow them to feel safe as I evolved into a version of me who I haven't been before – the version of me who you will hopefully get to meet as you now hold this book in your hands and read these pages?

Here are the ways that I navigated my dark night, which I hope may be able to help you too:

- I prayed for help and guidance and to understand what I was being shown in this time. My mantra was, 'Please help me to see what this is teaching me and what I can learn from this. Please help me to see what I need to see, hear what I need to hear and know what I need to know.'

- I sat with what I was feeling and welcomed it in and gave it a voice.
- I held myself and told myself that I was going to take care of me through it all.
- I held the younger afraid me who didn't feel worthy or enough and helped her to feel safe.
- I continued my daily rituals, even when they felt empty and pointless and meaningless – they were my anchor to the spiritual and helped keep my head above water.
- I didn't try to use logic for how I was feeling or force answers or outcomes or give it a story or meaning.
- I journaled, a lot. Even though I didn't want to write the words of how I was feeling, I got them down on paper so they were out of me, and I could process them this way.
- I got into nature, a lot, and sat with my favourite tree and told him all of my problems.
- I moved the emotions through my body through shaking, dancing and exercise.
- I went to my healers and trusted friends for support – those who I knew would just hold me through the process without trying to fix me.
- I cried, a lot.
- I wrote myself Post-it notes and stuck them all over my house as reminders. The one I have kept up until this day says, 'Remember who the f**k you are.'
- I didn't take my mind too seriously. When the noise and voice and doubts of my mind were loud, I kept going into the wisdom of my body. The fear wasn't there in my body, so

I knew that this was all coming from my ego mind and was something that needed to be processed, cleared and healed.

- I didn't panic about ruining my life by having this hard time and try to 'high vibe' my way out of it. I allowed it, knowing that this was just a season, and this too shall pass.

If you have already experienced your own dark night, I hope that this helps you to understand it in a different way. If not, I hope this prepares you should it happen for you. Whichever way, please don't panic about this – it's such a beautiful rite of passage on the spiritual journey.

Let's now move into how you can begin to embrace the unknown.

WHISPERS FROM YOUR SOUL

- Have you already experienced a dark night of the soul? Reflect on it here . . .
- What have the darkest times in your life taught you?
- How have your challenging experiences equipped you to help and support others going through the same?

‘It’s in the unknown spaces that your true purpose unfolds.’

Chapter 9

EMBRACE THE UNKNOWN

One of the only ways to live a life of true cosmic purpose is to learn to embrace the unknown, because it's in these unknown spaces that your true purpose unfolds.

There is no such thing as certainty in life, as much as your ego would love there to be. When we try to find those guarantees that things will work out in a certain way or we are assured of success before taking a risk, that's when we begin to struggle and push against life, and block all that wants to make its way to us as our ego self tries to find certainty and answers.

Our egos would rather stay in a familiar hell than move towards an uncertain heaven. You may try to argue that point with me and say that's silly and you'd never knowingly keep yourself somewhere that you were unhappy. Yet we do it over and over again by making the same choices and repeating the same behaviours that keep us trapped in the same cycles of dissatisfaction.

We then get to confirm our own bias that men can't be trusted, or nothing ever works out for me, or whatever the story is that you tell yourself about your familiar hell. We perpetuate our own cycles as we keep repeating them and stay in the known and familiar, even if it's not where we want to be.

So often, little human us – our ego self – wants to have it all figured out. We want certainty, guarantees and answers, and to know just what is happening and when. This comes from a place of control and fear. We especially, understandably, tend to feel fear around the unknown and, when we know that we really want something, but we don't quite know if, how or when it will work out, we want certainties, assurances and guarantees before we're willing to take the leap.

But, honestly, that's just not how life works. We can never be entirely certain of the future. The future is imagined. It doesn't exist yet. You are creating the future in this very moment, with every choice and thought and belief. It's in taking the leap that you learn all that you need to know to be able to land on the other side and hold what it is that you are creating. It's in taking that leap that you learn to trust in yourself and know that, no matter what happens, you can and will face it. What you face along the way of getting to your dream is helping you to grow into the version of you who can hold that dream.

The more you learn to trust yourself and allow the unique vibration of your soul to flow through you, the more you can move into the uncertainty of the unknown, as you know that, no matter what happens, you will be there for you and you can handle whatever it is that comes your way.

Sitting in the Unknown

You can begin to cultivate this trust by being there for yourself, especially in moments of uncertainty and anxiety, and not leaving yourself. When you abandon yourself in these moments and give in to the fears, drama and gripping and controlling of your ego, you leave the seat of your soul and the part of you that knows. Instead, sit with yourself in these moments and let yourself know that you are not going to leave you and you have got this. Even if it makes no sense right now and you don't know the answers and it's all unknown, trust that you can get through it no matter what it is. This is when you can allow yourself to sit in the unknown and allow the magic of the moment to unfold. Because, truly, all magic and miracles and blessings come out of the unknown.

In the moments of not knowing, anything is possible. Think about it – if you know what's happening next, you know, and that's what will happen. That's it; that's as good as it gets. But in the not knowing there are hundreds if not thousands of possibilities of what could happen, and many of those could be way better than you ever imagined.

The analogy I often use is this: imagine that you and I are together now and we know that we are going to a yoga class. That's it; that's what we're doing – we're going to a yoga class, which will probably be lovely. But imagine if instead we embraced the unknown and all of its possibilities. We decided that we'd leave where we were now and intuitively feel into whether we wanted to turn left or right. Then we'd look for a sign, and we saw something ahead that said 'this way' so we followed it. And we kept doing that, embracing the unknown and going with the flow – we could end up in Bali. I'm serious! Rather than a yoga class in the local leisure centre, we could end up in tropical paradise.

Of course, I am kind of joking. But my point is that, in the unknown, anything becomes possible and, by allowing yourself to surrender into the unknown, which may feel scary to begin with, life opens up so many other possibilities that your ego mind may never have even considered.

You also stunt so much of your soul growth by trying to live in the confines of the known. You may think it feels safer, but it restricts so much of your growth. If you knew for absolute sure what the outcome would be, there would be no need to expand into more of yourself or push out of your comfort zone or do something that scares or challenges you and makes you believe more in yourself, helping you to grow into this braver, more trusting version of you. If there were a guarantee, there would be no growth.

It's in the moments of letting go of the certainty that we are able to allow ourselves to be guided towards what is waiting for us. Learn to leap into the unknown, even if it makes no sense – that's when life will begin to catch you and show you that it gets even better than you could ever even have imagined. Learn to trust it, even if it makes no sense.

Me giving up my very good job in the corporate world made absolutely no sense and was a huge leap into the unknown, but it's a leap I am so grateful I took. When I gave up my entire life in London to move to a place in the country I hadn't even seen and that was up for sale, it was entirely unknown, but, as I allowed life to unfold around me, it has taken care of me time after time. Each time I leap, the universe catches me – and it will catch you too. But you have to take that leap into the unknown for that to happen. You have to move away from the so-called safe shore.

You will live your entire life in the comfort zone of your ego if you don't learn to sit in and embrace the discomfort of the unknown, and trust yourself and your soul enough to move beyond it into all that's waiting for you.

Now that you've learned to embrace the unknown, let's explore how to begin to live from the inside out and make yourself the centre of your universe.

WHISPERS FROM YOUR SOUL

- ❍ Where in your life do you stay in a familiar hell rather than moving to an uncertain heaven?
- ❍ Why do you fear the unknown so much?
- ❍ In what areas of life do you most try to grip, control and micromanage, and force an outcome?

‘Begin to live from the inside out and vibrate with the frequency of your soul self.’

Chapter 10

LIVE FROM THE INSIDE OUT

One thing that will shift you further into your cosmic purpose is learning to live from the inside out rather than from the outside in.

When you live from the outside in, you allow the world around you and all that happens out there to determine your inner state and whether you can be happy, fulfilled, purposeful or in flow. Your whole day can be ruined by someone being rude to you, something inconvenient happening or seeing something you don't like on social media.

When you allow the outside world to determine your reality and emotional state, you will always be at the mercy of an external force, and life uncertainties will throw you out of alignment over and over again. You take on other people's opinions, moods and energies, and find yourself in constant comparison.

When you are waiting for something out there to happen or change before you can be happy, you'll wait forever: 'When I finally get that relationship I'll be happy'; 'When I finally get that promotion I'll be happy'. You give away the power to live your cosmic purpose to the outside world. You end up chasing but never attaining, striving but never arriving.

Living in this way means that you are fully dependent on the outside world for approval, validation, answers, a sense of worth and to fulfil your emotional needs and give you what you need. You are looking to the outside word to give you purpose, meaning and a sense of self, which it never can. All of this comes from within you; it truly is an inside job.

When you live from the inside out, you are anchored in your essence, your truth, yourself and your soul. You know that you are cosmic consciousness, a part of the divine. You know your own power, worth and purpose. You find a deep acceptance and appreciation for yourself. You allow your soul rather than the outside world to guide you and you listen more to your inner world than the outer noise. You begin to allow your soul to live and experience life through you and you start to truly understand the concept of being a soul having a human experience.

You also come to understand that the outer world is a direct reflection of your inner world and that your inner world creates your outer reality. If you believe that the world is a scary, uncertain place, that people can't be trusted or that things always go wrong, then that is exactly what you're going to see manifest in the outside world. We don't see things as they are; we see them as we are.

As soon as you realise that it all begins within you and anything that you want to see happen or manifest in the outside world first needs to come from within you, your entire sense of reality begins to change. You realise that everything that you seek – love, happiness, approval, abundance, acceptance, purpose and peace – cannot come from the outside world; it must come from within you first. You realise that you are a powerful co-creator, and you are constantly creating your reality from the inside out.

Making Yourself the Centre of Your Universe

If you want to see abundance in the outside world, you first need to feel and create that sense of abundance on the inside and truly feel abundant in yourself (remembering that abundance doesn't necessarily mean money – it's joy, happiness, laughter, connection, things falling into place; it's all that the universe wants to offer you).

If you want love and connection in the outside world, you first need to find love and connection within you. Whatever you want to see manifest on the outside first has to be present on the inside – if you want people to respect you, you need to respect yourself; if you want people to choose you, you have to choose yourself; if you want people to love you, you have to love yourself.

Begin to live from the inside out and vibrate with the frequency of your soul self and what it is that you want in your life – remember that everything in the world is energy and attracts a vibrational match. Einstein said, 'Everything is energy and that's all there is to it. Match the frequency of the reality you want and you cannot help but get that reality. It can be no other way. This is not philosophy. This is physics.'

The answer to the changes you want to make, the stability you're seeking, the answers you are looking for, the direction you need to go in and all that you want to see happen in your life is all within you. It always was. You've just been taught to look outside of you, but it's time to bring it back and begin to live from the inside out.

If you don't like the way someone is treating you or the way something is working out in the outside world, don't try to change them on the outside, go within and make those changes within you. Rather than wishing they didn't treat you like that and believing that you'd be able to be happy if only they would change their behaviour, go within and look at the part of you that is bothered by it or allows it and ask why. Perhaps you've allowed people to treat you a certain way as, deep down, you didn't believe that you deserved any better. Work on your self-esteem and self-worth and you will automatically create better boundaries, stand and speak up for yourself more and carry yourself through life in a different way. This means that you will no longer attract or allow this kind of energy in your life and these same things won't affect you in the same way again.

If you don't like the way that your life is currently, stop waiting for the outside world to change and look within you at the part of you that isn't happy with your life – examine why and start to change that. Perhaps you're living too much from your ego wanting things to be a different way or this is a nudge from your soul as you're ignoring your path and straying in the wrong direction.

If you want anything in your life to change, you first need to look inside and make those changes within you. Nothing changes until you change. Change your inner world and the outer world will naturally begin to change too. This may mean working on deeper levels of self-worth and self-approval or finding an inner strength that helps you to set better boundaries.

As you begin to take back your power and focus on your inner world, a powerful shift will take place. You get to determine who you are and what matters to you. You get to live the life that you want to live. You no longer need to conform to ideals, and the world and other people can continue to do what they need to do without it affecting you and your inner world.

When you love and accept all of yourself and your quirks, your uniqueness and your ways, you won't need the outside world for it. You won't need the outside world to give you anything that you cannot find within yourself – and that's when life truly becomes magical.

The outside world is ever-changing and other people are always going to throw us curveballs, test us, challenge us and perhaps not behave in quite the way we want them to. If your happiness or sense of self is dependent on any person, place or thing outside of you, it can always be taken away and therefore your sense of worth, self, happiness and purpose go with it. Because, unless that happiness is already within you, the outer world can only give it to you temporarily. Your sense of happiness will then disappear if that outer thing ever changes.

That's not to say that you can't have nice or material things. It's often a misconception that to live a spiritual life means to live a life of poverty or denial. Have the nice car or house or handbag or clothes if that's what you want, providing that they are not the source of your happiness and, if that thing disappeared, your sense of self would not go with it. You need to know who you are on the inside, not because of what you have on the outside. In fact, once you become happy, all of these things will naturally begin to come to you, but the beautiful thing is that you won't actually need them anymore and they will just add to your already happy and fulfilled life.

So, begin to manage your own inner frequency – rather than getting caught in the doubts and fears of your mind or the outside world, notice when you are stuck in stories, thought patterns or loops and trying to gain what you want from outside you. Instead, drop into your higher heart and let your soul essence expand within you. Remember that this is your inner world, and you get to be the one who creates how you feel and who and what you allow to affect you.

Close your eyes. Go within. Don't let your ego jump to the past or future. In this moment, right here, right now, you have absolutely everything that you need within you. Be present with that, with your inner world. It's only your ego that looks to the outside world for approval or fulfilment. Keep dropping into the presence of your inner world and your soul. Create the kind of world and life you want in your inner world, and you'll begin to see it reflected on the outside.

You're still going to have bad days and days when it doesn't flow, but you're not going to take it personally and feel like the world is against you. Instead, you're going to be able to look within at what is happening in your inner landscape and where you're out of connection, flow and alignment with yourself.

You need to create an inner world in which you believe in and back yourself. A world in which you feel your dreams are alive and real and possible within you. A world in which you know you are here on this earth at this time for a great purpose, and that you and your dreams are so needed. Creating what you want first in your inner world will help you to easily be able to create and manifest whatever you want into the reality of your outer world.

Begin to live from the inside out and your entire world will change. Make yourself the centre of your universe. Begin to live from the inside out and vibrate with the frequency of your soul self and what it is that you want in your life – remember that everything in the world is energy and attracts a vibrational match.

Now that you've come to understand that it's an inside job and your inner world creates your outer, you can take radical responsibility for your own life.

WHISPERS FROM YOUR SOUL

- ❍ Where do you live from the outside in, looking to the world around you for happiness, approval and to give you what you need?
- ❍ Where are you waiting for the outside world to change before you can have what you want or be who you want to be?
- ❍ How can you begin to live from the inside out and self-source what you are looking for?

‘As soon as you accept your part to play, you take back your power to make changes.’

Chapter 11

TAKE RADICAL RESPONSIBILITY FOR YOUR OWN LIFE

One of the most challenging but transformative parts of this journey is taking radical responsibility for your life.

If you want to truly step into your cosmic purpose and claim your own life, you need to come to understand that you have a part to play in everything that happens in your life. I sometimes long for the days when I could blame everyone else for how I was feeling or why things weren't working out for me, and it was my boss's fault or my partner's fault or the traffic's fault that I felt the way I did. Life seemed so much 'easier' back then, in the days when I could play the blame game and it was always someone else's fault.

But the whole time you blame anything outside of you, you give your power away to that person or situation and have to wait for that to change before you can. You strangle your cosmic purpose, making your life about others and something outside of you rather than the journey of your soul.

As soon as you accept your part to play in anything that you are going through, you take back your power to make changes and, instead of asking, 'Why is this happening to me?' or 'Why are they doing that to me?', you get to ask, 'What can I learn from this, what is this showing me and how can I grow from this?' You begin to see everything in life as happening *for* you not *to* you, which helps you to learn, grow and evolve on your soul path towards your cosmic purpose.

It's important to realise that no one can make you feel anything unless you allow them to. The late, great Dr Wayne Dyer used to say, 'You can't squeeze an orange without getting orange juice.' I remember being really confused by this when I first heard it, but, over time, it made so much sense. If there is no anger within you, no one can squeeze it out of you; if there is no jealousy within you, no one can squeeze it out of you; if there is no pain within you, no one can squeeze it out of you.

So, rather than blaming others for squeezing what is already within you, go within and begin to heal those wounds that are causing you to feel the way you do.

Healing Your Inner World

When you notice yourself affected by someone else's actions or words, take a pause and use this as a beautiful opportunity for some inner exploration and to get to know yourself in a deeper way. Question how it made you feel and why. Don't give the power to them for making you feel that way. Take back your power by acknowledging the parts of you that reacted in that way and examine why. You are responsible for how you react to every single thing that anyone says or does or anything that happens in your life and, once you realise that, you get to respond rather than react.

If someone is not messaging you back or behaving in the way that you want them to or your boss is being mean to you, it is not their fault that you feel anxious, sad or unhappy. It's yours, because there is a part of you that wants or expects things to be different to the way they are or is allowing the behaviour of others. Look at why you need things to be a certain way, why you keep allowing yourself to be treated the same way or how you're allowing yourself to be influenced by things outside you.

As you begin to do this, you will no longer keep attracting these same situations and lessons over and over as you will finally be learning, healing and freeing the parts of you that attract them in the first place. Because, whether we like to believe it or not, we do keep attracting the same things into our lives over and over until we take responsibility for why we are doing this and heal our inner world rather than trying to force or wait for something or someone in the outer world to change before we can be happy and free.

Giving up blame is such an important part of this. Stop blaming anyone or anything outside you for the way that your life is – this strips you of all your power and makes you a victim, and you are no victim. You are a powerful soul with a cosmic purpose to fulfil and this is your life. When you blame others, you give away your power to create change in your own life.

Instead, look at these places in your life and ask yourself what your part was to play in the situation and how you contributed to it. This shifts the power back to you and puts things back in your control. I know this isn't easy – we never want to feel like we played a part in the challenging, tough parts of our lives or in the things that go wrong; it's much easier for it to be someone else's fault. But once you accept that radical responsibility for the part you had to play, you take back your power to change things in your life because the only person who can ever truly make change in your life is you. No one else can do it for you. I can't, this book can't. You may read it and nod along, but you, yes YOU, are the only one who can actually change your life. Know that you can change your life in any moment that you choose to, and we'll look at how to do that in the next chapter.

I want to end this chapter with a little reminder that you are not responsible for anyone else's life, problems or happiness. Everyone is on their own individual journey and each one of us is only responsible for our own lives. You cannot fix, heal or rescue anyone, as much as you might want to. You cannot change anyone who doesn't want to be changed. You cannot save anyone from their own life experiences or rock bottoms or dark nights of the soul. All you can do is be there to support and love them when they need it. Sometimes, this also means knowing when it's time to set boundaries, put yourself first or walk away and love someone from afar. Taking radical responsibility for your own life also means giving everyone else radical responsibility for theirs.

WHISPERS FROM YOUR SOUL

- ❍ Where in your life are you blaming, complaining and making excuses?
- ❍ Where do you need to take back responsibility for your life and how are you going to begin to do this?
- ❍ Where and how do you make yourself responsible for other people's lives and happiness and try to fix, heal and rescue?

'If you don't like something in your life, you have the power to make different choices and change it.'

Chapter 12

YOU ALWAYS HAVE A CHOICE

You always have a choice in life. Not always in what happens to you (even though we could argue that our soul chooses every experience to help us to learn, grow and evolve), but you always have a choice in how you act, react, think and feel about a situation or circumstance.

In any moment, you can choose to keep doing things the way you've always done them, think the things you've always thought and behave in the way you've always behaved or . . . you can choose to do it differently.

You can choose to see all that isn't going right, all that could go wrong, all the reasons it may not work out and listen to the doubts and fears of your ego mind. Or you could choose to look at what could go right, what could be possible and how it could all work out and to see it all from the higher perspective of your soul.

If you are always looking at what is going wrong, what isn't working, how things aren't fair or right, or you are living and acting from your subconscious limiting beliefs and fears, that is all you will ever see in life and more of the same will keep happening.

As soon as you begin to realise the power of your thoughts,

words and beliefs and how they shape your reality, you can begin to choose new thoughts, new words and new beliefs and that will begin to create real change in your life.

Choosing Thoughts and Beliefs that Empower Your Soul

It may not feel like it, but you can choose your thoughts. Think about how easy you find it to choose not to believe something good that someone says about you or that something good is about to happen for you. You can do the same with the negative thoughts – you can choose not to allow them to be true for you.

When you change your thoughts, you will begin to change your life. So, begin to choose thoughts that empower you, that expand your vision and open you up to all the possibilities. Choose happy thoughts, good feeling thoughts and thoughts that help you to make new, brave, bold decisions, and believe in what could go right and how it could all work out.

Create more thoughts around what you desire, more thoughts that are supportive of your values and that help you to know and believe in your worth and trust yourself. Notice when you get stuck in thought spirals of 'not enough' and, as you practised in Chapter 7, flip those thoughts to ones that are loving, kind, supportive and encouraging and that bring you peace.

When you catch your mind telling you that you aren't good enough, tell yourself that you are more than enough just the way you are. If you find yourself fixating on something you don't like about yourself, find three things that you do like. Talk to and praise yourself, constantly telling yourself what you have done well and how proud you are of yourself, especially when you do something brave or out of your comfort zone.

You can also choose your beliefs. You can choose to believe that everything is working in your favour and for your own highest good, or you can choose to believe that life is against you and nothing ever works out. You can choose to believe that you are capable of anything you set your mind to and will find a way to make it work, or you can choose to believe that things aren't possible for you and you'd never be able to make it happen anyway. As Henry Ford once said, 'Whether you think you can, or you think you can't – you're right.'

The more you begin to choose thoughts and beliefs that empower you, the more you will expand your mind beyond limitations, see things differently and look for the possibilities and opportunities that surround you. As this happens, you will naturally begin to make different choices in your life and lifestyle that back up your new beliefs, helping you to make changes and live a more soul-led existence.

You'll realise that, if you don't like something in your life, you have the power to make different choices and change it. You may tell me that you can't just change your job. That you'd like to move into something that gives you more purpose, but you need to pay the bills and have responsibilities, and so this could feel like you don't have a choice – but this is where you give your power away.

Make this your choice. You could choose to quit your job, but right now you are choosing to stay because the security of the pay cheque outweighs the desire of being in a more aligned role – for now. As soon as you make this your choice, you take back your power over the situation and things will automatically begin to shift. And while you're choosing to stay in the job, change your attitude towards it and how you approach it. Choose to see this time as an opportunity to learn more about yourself and grow in some way so that you will be ready when the time comes to leave.

The same applies to any other areas of your life – for example, if you don't like being single, change the way you look at it and instead choose to see this as an opportunity to get to know and love yourself so that you can be ready for when your person arrives. Get clear on who and what you want and become that person for yourself, as this shift alone will bring your person closer.

Choose to see whatever you are currently going through as an opportunity to learn more about yourself and life, and gathering and learning what you need to grow into more of what you want. Keep choosing to listen to the whispers of your heart and soul over the doubts and fears of your mind. Choose to trust and believe rather than shrinking back into the so-called safety of your comfort zone. Choose faith over fear and just wait and see how your life begins to change.

Because every choice that you make in life is creating your future and opening new avenues, opportunities and possibilities, and moving you into a different timeline – including the choices that you are not making. Because not making a choice about something is also a choice, and often one of the most painful ones.

If you get honest, you'll start to realise that the times when you feel the most stuck, trapped, restricted and out of alignment in your life are the times when you are not making a choice about something. You are operating from fear, seeing yourself as a victim or waiting for something or someone outside of you to make the decision for you. You are keeping yourself stuck in indecision – and this is one of the powerless and trapped places to be in life.

As soon as you make a choice, either way, you can then begin to align with the pathway of that choice and take the first steps. Once you do this, your soul will begin to guide you. You can't make a wrong choice as long as you are making one, as there is then movement rather than stagnancy, and life can once more begin to weave through you. Even if you make mistakes along the way, there is no such thing as a mistake if you learn from it.

You can also choose to change your decisions, change your direction, change your opinion, change your beliefs and change your mind at any time you choose to. How freeing is that? Once you begin to realise that you always have a choice, your life opens up in so many new ways, all of which you get to choose.

That's not to say that any of this is easy. Choosing to believe a new thought is uncomfortable; pushing beyond a limiting belief is uncomfortable; facing a fear is uncomfortable; holding a boundary is uncomfortable; doing something differently to what people have expected from you for so long is uncomfortable; saying no is uncomfortable. But it's in this discomfort that growth happens, and you become who you're here to be.

So, begin to make those new choices, even if they feel uncomfortable. If something in your life hasn't been working, choose to do it differently. You can choose, right now, to keep doing things the way you've always done them and stay stuck in old ways. Or make that one choice, today, that will open up a whole new world for you that is more aligned with your soul.

Choose to believe that your soul has chosen this very experience for you to help you to evolve, grow and expand into more of your cosmic purpose – and your soul wouldn't choose anything that you couldn't get through. This, in my opinion, is one of the most powerful choices you will ever make in life.

Remember though, although our soul may have chosen certain things for us and we have our own choices, we can't choose or control how other people behave or act towards us or what choices they make. Those people may be living completely from ego and out of alignment with their path and soul, and this is where we do have a choice – we can choose how much we let their behaviour affect us and how long we continue to allow it in our lives. We don't have to believe that our souls chose it and therefore we must stay and allow ourselves to be hurt or disrespected over and over again.

Our souls also know when the lesson is complete and when to walk away, and the more you learn to know and trust yourself, the easier that will be. You can choose to blame and wish the situation was different and give all of your power away to that person or situation outside of you. Or you can choose to deepen into your soul self and stand in your power and worth, knowing who you are and what you deserve.

I want to end this chapter by sharing with you one of the most profound choices I learned early on in my spiritual journey: choose to be kind rather than right. It sounds simple enough, but this one choice will really start to show you whether you are living from your ego or your soul. Your ego wants to be right, at all costs. It will fight, argue and try to convince you that being kind isn't the right option and that you are, in fact, right. In any moments that you can, choose to be kind rather than right. This one choice will take you closer to your soul.

You know now that you always have a choice, and you can choose the role of your soul. It's time to begin to listen to those whispers from your soul.

WHISPERS FROM YOUR SOUL

- ❍ Do you want to keep being this version of yourself? Do you want to keep having these thoughts and believing these beliefs? Because you can choose not to, at any time.
- ❍ Who are you going to choose to be?
- ❍ Where do you need to begin to make new or different choices in your life, or even just a choice about something?

‘When you learn to follow the whispers from your soul, life becomes a magical, soul-led adventure.’

Chapter 13

LISTEN TO THE WHISPERS FROM YOUR SOUL

Your soul is always trying to speak to you, whispering you forwards into more and more of yourself and calling you into your highest vibration. That little nudge you get to apply for a new job, speak up about something or no longer keep accepting a behaviour is your soul gently guiding you forwards into more of your cosmic purpose.

These whispers from your soul, particularly in the beginning, may also come through the more 'negative' feelings, such as despair, frustration, sadness, anger and loneliness, as very often this is the only way that we will listen and your soul is trying to get you to pay attention.

It's often only when we are hit by these big emotions that we stop merely existing and take a good look at our lives and all that isn't making us happy or fulfilled. It's in these moments that we begin to see how far we have strayed from ourselves and our soul, and this is the first step of being able to bring yourself back and listen to the whispers of your soul calling you home to more of your cosmic purpose.

Very often, we get confused between the voice of our ego and the voice of our soul and, as our ego often shouts the loudest, that's the one we get used to listening to the most.

The voice of your ego is usually heard and comes more from your head. It's noisy, urgent and often fear-based, giving mixed messages and lots of reasons to worry and doubt. It's all about 'should's and 'shouldn't's and 'if's and 'maybe's and has you going round and round over the same thing in different ways.

The voice of your soul is more of a felt sense. It comes from somewhere deeper in your body and is calm, loving and consistent. It's clear, direct, uses very few words and feels supportive, if a little scary.

You see, the voice of your soul is the inconvenient voice of truth that tells you to do the one thing that's been scaring you or that you've been avoiding, as facing that thing is what will help you to grow into the version of you who you need to be to welcome what comes next.

It tells you things that don't make logical sense to your ego mind and perhaps everyone else around you. Your soul wants you to step into the fullness of who you came here to be and follow the road less travelled on your soul journey. This journey may challenge you, it will certainly change you and it will help you to learn and grow and expand in the ways that you need to.

Your ego wants to protect you and keep you caged in your comfort zone. It wants certainty. It wants approval and validation from others and for you to fit in and be accepted at all costs. It worries about doing something wrong or what others will think about what you're doing.

Your soul wants to free you and guide you towards your

unique soul destiny and what your soul came here to do in this lifetime. Your soul doesn't worry about what others may think or say, or whether it even makes any sense to the outside world. Your soul simply wants you to be you and live the life that you came here to live. And, to help you to do that, your soul will constantly whisper to you, 'This way, over here, this is where you need to be.'

Tuning Into the Voice of Your Soul

In the beginning, it may be hard to hear or trust these little whispers. But, over time, the more you listen to and follow this inner guidance, the more you will be able to follow your soul to where it wants to lead you, and this is when life becomes a magical, soul-led adventure.

Part of the problem with hearing the voice of your soul in the beginning is that you've gone so far away that you can barely hear it. The more you try to be someone you're not, the more you shrink your cosmic self, and the further you get from your soul's path, the quieter the voice of your soul becomes as you drown it out to listen to the shouting of your ego, or other people's. But your soul never left you; it's always there, patiently waiting to guide you back on your path whenever you're ready to listen.

This journey back to hearing your inner whispers begins by doing just that: listening. Let your soul know that you are ready to hear this inner guidance and carve out quiet time to just go within and listen. When you have a big decision to make or you feel uncertain about something, see if you can drop beneath the noise of your ego mind into a quiet place within and listen to your soul.

At first, you may hear nothing, but, over time, you'll feel a little nudge in your belly, a knowing deep within or an expansion in your heart, or you'll hear a little whisper. The way that our souls speak is going to be different for each one of us and you need to take time to get used to how your soul speaks to you.

And then you need to trust and start to follow your soul's guidance. This is often the missing piece. It's through following the whispers and guidance that you will begin to develop the trust in your soul and yourself. As you get braver and bolder and begin to live by your soul's whispers, your soul will speak to you even more, guiding you towards so many more opportunities and expansions.

You'll begin to trust that, even if the initial soul nudge feels scary and unknown and you don't know the 'how's, none of that matters and the journey will unfold perfectly before you as you take the first steps.

One thing that is often true about your soul's whispers is that they very often make no logical sense to either your ego mind or the world around you. And they're not meant to. As you listen to the whispers of your soul, you are guided towards new experiences, lessons and opportunities that are out of your comfort zone as they are helping you to expand into all that your soul knows you are capable of.

Over the years, I've learned that the less sense an intuitive nudge makes, the more I know I need to trust and follow it. I have the benefit of experience now, but I can honestly say that, even if there have been sticky bits in between and doubts, following these whispers has always led me to something better than I can even imagine.

We tell ourselves that if we feel scared to make a big move, it must mean that it isn't the right thing, but that couldn't be further from the truth. There is a big difference between an ego fear that feels anxiety-inducing, nervy and uncertain, and the fear of following a soul call that is calling you into expansion, even if that feels uncomfortable and unknown.

If following the whispers from your soul was easy, there would be no growth, no evolution and no need for you to push beyond the fears of the ego mind to take you to where your soul wants to be. This is all part of the journey, so turn towards your fears and no longer allow them to hold you back – we'll explore facing your fears in the next chapter.

Remember that every dream and desire that stirs within you, every intuitive nudge that your soul self gives you, is taking you further along your path and helping you to know, trust and expand into yourself even more.

Connecting to your higher heart

Before we close this chapter, I want to introduce you to your higher heart, as this is often the place from which your soul whispers to you, hoping that you will hear.

We are often told to 'listen to our heart', but this can sometimes cause difficulties if our hearts have been broken or betrayed and we have closed off or added layers of protection around them. When your heart chakra is closed or blocked, you will find it hard to trust yourself (or others/the universe), feel unworthy, lonely or isolated, stuck in the past and struggling to move forwards, and afraid to fully commit to what you want in case it doesn't work out.

This can add to the confusion we feel around making big decisions or deeply trusting our intuition as our human heart can sometimes try to make us cautious or want to keep us protected from further pain, disappointment or abandonment. This can cause us to try to grip, control and manage life in order to avoid hurt, pain or disappointment, but, in doing so, you actually end up disconnecting yourself from your higher heart and the guidance of your soul. It's then extremely difficult to live from a place of 'feeling' and trusting your intuition and inner knowing when these feelings are coming from a wounded heart, continuing to keep you in patterns and cycles from the past. This is when it's vital to begin to connect to your higher heart, also known as the seat of the soul.

Your thymus chakra, or the ascended heart chakra, is located between the throat and the heart and connects you to your higher self, helping you to remember more of who you are. It is where your soul purpose and power are located, and working with this chakra will help you to align with higher levels of spiritual consciousness and your soul path in life.

It's your higher heart that you want to learn to listen to over your cautious human heart, so that you can fully begin to listen to your soul whispers and live from your heart, allowing your soul self to begin to shine through.

Start the work of healing your heart. To do this, you need to begin to heal all that keeps your heart closed, cautious and protected. Be honest about where and why you don't trust your heart or keep yourself closed off or protected to avoid hurt, pain and disappointment. Forgive, soften and open your heart once again. Look at where things from your past are affecting your ability to be able to live in trust, surrender and connection so that you can begin to live from your higher heart and allow your soul to live and speak through you.

WHISPERS FROM YOUR SOUL

- Do you tend to listen more to the doubts of your ego mind or the whispers of your soul?
- How does your soul speak to you? What does it feel like when you get those intuitive nudges of guidance from your soul? Think of a time when you followed a soul nudge. What happened? Think of a time when you ignored a soul nudge and listened to your ego fears. What happened?
- How do you keep your heart shut down, closed off and protected, and why? How can you begin the healing process to open your heart and be able to access the wisdom of your higher heart?

‘When you are in connection to your soul self, you realise that there is nothing to fear but fear itself and that you are always being guided and protected.’

Chapter 14

FACE YOUR FEARS

You cannot live a life of cosmic purpose without feeling, recognising, facing and overcoming your fears. Living a life of growth, evolution and transformation means that there are going to be times when you feel fear – it's natural; you haven't been this version of you before or stepped into this version of your life before.

Facing your fears isn't about no longer having fears, but about trusting yourself enough to know that, no matter what happens, you can turn to face them and overcome them. It's knowing what your fears are, turning towards them and no longer allowing them to silently control you and stop you from living the life of your dreams.

Your fears will stop you over and over again if you allow them to. Every time you take a step out of your comfort zone and begin to move forwards, they will be waiting, hiding around the corner to jump out at you and push you back. They will keep you stuck in your comfort zone, repeating old patterns and feeling frustrated because, deep down, you know there is more to life.

There is a big difference between a true no from your soul and an ego fear that wants to keep you stuck in your comfort zone. A soul no will be like when you're about to touch something hot or step out into the road when something is coming. It will be a clear, decisive, quick no. Ego fear is anxiety-inducing; it comes in waves and whispers to you of all that could go wrong or why it won't work out. It feels icky, scary and frustrating, especially because there is a part of you that knows you should be going for it and saying yes.

Our egos fight the most and shout the loudest when we are on the edge of a huge soul breakthrough, evolution or awakening. Your ego fears the death of itself and doesn't want to lose control over you or for you to evolve into a higher awareness and consciousness and begin to listen more to your soul. So it will fight and fight to try to maintain control, usually by making you afraid to keep you 'safe' and small.

Very often, when you are just about to take the leap, make a big change, follow the soul nudge or do something you've never done before, the big fears come up that stop you leaping for a dream or that tell you it's not a good idea, and you convince yourself that, because you feel afraid, it's a sign you shouldn't do it. In fact, it's in these moments when you should because, as you push beyond this fear, that same thing will never scare you again.

Many of your biggest fears come from not trusting you, life, your soul or the universe enough, and so the voice of your ego manages to shout louder and convince you to stay where you are. Yet, every time you give into a fear and allow it to hold you back, you give power to that fear and make it bigger than yourself, your soul and the universe. You choose fear over faith.

But did you know that an estimated 91 per cent of what we worry about never comes true? And in studies it was shown that of the worries that did come true, participants found that they handled the problem better than they thought they could or learned a valuable lesson from what happened.[1]

This just shows that you never know what you are truly capable of until you face and move beyond a big fear. In doing so, you overcome a part of your ego and move into even deeper trust and alignment with your soul. When you are in connection to your soul self, the divine part of you, you realise that there is nothing to fear but fear itself and that you are always being guided and protected.

I've had to lean into deep trust and face fears so many times on my journey – from my initial big leap to give up a 'safe' and well-paid job in the corporate world to go to India and become a yoga teacher, to continuing to talk about the moon all those years ago when no one was listening and I was regularly ridiculed for it, to giving up all of my 'safe' corporate and private yoga clients in London a few years ago to write books.

To this day, speaking in front of big crowds and doing live TV and radio scares me. Imagine if I listened to those fears and didn't push beyond them. You would likely not be holding this book in your hands, and I wouldn't be able to share my work with you and the world. Part of my purpose is overcoming those fears, or at least not allowing them to hold me back, as that's the only way I get to spread my message. I can truthfully say to you that each time I have faced and overcome a fear, my life has expanded and evolved in a way that I can't even imagine, and I trust me and my soul so deeply now.

You cannot keep waiting for a future moment when you won't be scared to make a move, make a change or make a dream come true – this moment will never come and you'll be waiting your whole life. There is always going to be a fear to push beyond when you are expanding into a next level of you and life, and pushing beyond this fear is part of the journey.

If you truly want to live a life of cosmic purpose and connection to your soul and make a difference in the world, you need to stop being afraid to do things differently to the way things have always been done or to do something new, or at least not let that fear stop you.

Pushing Beyond Your Fears

The first step to overcoming your fears is to begin to notice what they are and what the voice of your ego is telling you. What is it that you are so afraid of around making the changes in your life that you know you need to make or doing the things that you really feel you want to do?

It may be a fear of what others may say or think or whether you'll be able to make it work or what might go wrong. It may be a fear of rejection or abandonment or failing, of not being good enough or losing control. Maybe you have a fear of change or uncertainty. Once you realise what your deepest fears are, you'll begin to realise that it's that same fear (in slightly different disguises) that has held you back from so many opportunities in life.

If you're struggling to identify your deep fears, look at where you repeat patterns or feel frustrations about the same things not working out in your life. Next, see if you can look at where these fears come from. Where did they first begin? Are they yours, society's or the voice of someone else? Maybe you're hearing the voice of a well-meaning parent or caregiver or ex-partner or teacher. I know that when I was quitting my job to go to India, my grandparents in particular were so afraid for me and what it meant to give up a good job, as you just didn't do that in their generation. Perhaps you're listening to an old version of you who hasn't quite caught up with who you are now or a societal expectation of how life should be.

Now, be aware of what that fear is trying to keep you safe from. Your ego and your fears are not enemies to be beaten, they are parts of you to integrate and overcome. They are just trying to keep you safe in their own way and prevent you from failing or being rejected or abandoned. But they don't know how much you have changed and grown and how capable you are now. So, lean into your soul self and tell these fears: 'Thank you so much for trying to keep me safe, but I don't need you anymore. I've got this, our soul's got this and I'm going to take it from here. I trust me; you can trust me.'

Then take one step towards your fears and I promise, once you do this, they will lose their power over you and never hold you back in the same way again. Face your fears, don't let them control you anymore and, instead, find a deep, unwavering trust in yourself and where your soul is calling you to go. On the other side of all of your doubts, fears and insecurities is the life that you have been waiting for, and it's the journey through overcoming these that will help you to grow into the version of you who is ready for that life.

Remember that both faith and fear require you to believe in something that you can't see. You need to allow your faith to become bigger than your fear.

A final note before I close this chapter on something that many people fear: death. Death is not what we should fear. What we should fear even more is not living while we are alive and allowing fear to control us, hold us back and miss opportunities and all that life has to offer. Death is one of the only certainties in life – it's going to happen to us all and, depending on your beliefs, it's only the ending of this chapter of your life; your soul is eternal and never dies. Anytime that you are allowing a fear to hold you back, consider the possibility of not allowing yourself to fully embrace this life and all that your soul wants you to experience – it may just change the way you allow your fears to control you.

I'm so proud of you for facing and overcoming your fears. And it's from here that you can begin to find the faith to meet the universe halfway (and surrender the rest).

WHISPERS FROM YOUR SOUL

- What is your biggest fear(s)?
- Where has this fear come from and what is it trying to keep you safe from? Can you see how this same fear has held you back so many times in your life?
- What one step could you take today to lean into trust in your soul and overcome this fear?

'Know that the universe has heard you, your soul has a plan and, as long as you have done all that you can, this or something better is coming your way.'

Chapter 15

MEET THE UNIVERSE HALFWAY (AND THEN SURRENDER THE REST)

Very often, there is confusion as to whether you should be doing all that you can to make a soul dream come true and really going after what you want or trusting your soul's path, surrendering to the universe and allowing it to come to you. The truth is somewhere in the middle – you have to meet the universe halfway.

It's important to remember that we are never given a dream or desire without also being given the means to achieve it. It's also true that every dream and desire within you is there because it's part of what the world needs and only you can bring it to life.

But you cannot simply throw a dream, desire or intention out there into the universe and think you've done enough and just expect it to happen. This is what I mean by meeting the universe halfway – you also have to put in the required changes, effort, focus and energy. You do what you can do and play your part and then you surrender the rest and allow the universe to play its part. Both of these parts are important and vital to a life of cosmic purpose and living the life that your soul wants for you.

Playing Your Part

First, you need to play your part, and this is often the hardest bit. Many people say that they want this or that, but they aren't necessarily willing to make the changes and do the uncomfortable, challenging or expanding things that it takes to get to where they want to go.

For example, if you want to manifest a new job, are you sending out CVs or actively looking for that job? If you want to manifest a partner or friendships, are you putting yourself out there and in situations where you can meet new people? If you want to manifest purpose, are you spending time doing things and with people that make you purposeful? Are you truly doing all that you can do to make what you want to happen come to life? Do you need to study something, prepare in some way or lay any foundations in you so that you're ready to hold it when it arrives?

We tend to sit back and wait for what we want to simply come to us and then declare that manifestation 'doesn't work', or our intentions never come true, and that life doesn't work for us. We stay stuck in jobs, relationships and situations that aren't bringing our souls to life, so we feel even more purposeless and small and stuck. This is such a huge form of ego self-sabotage.

You also need to look at where you get in your own way – the resistances and obstacles that you put in the way – and discover what your blocks are to your manifestations. Do you truly believe that you are worthy and deserving of what you want and that you can have it? If you don't, and there are any doubts or fears within you around bringing your dreams and desires to life, these will block your manifestations and, each time the universe delivers, you will sabotage it and perpetuate your own story that you can't have it. Your ego is sneaky like that.

You need to do all that you can to make what you want happen. Then you leave the 'how's, the 'when's, the 'what's, the 'why's and the 'who's to the universe. Leave your ego and its time-frames and preferences and demands out of the way. You've done what you can, and then you surrender the rest.

Surrendering to the Universe

This part is important as otherwise you strangle the flow of your manifestation by trying to exert your will on it and control the 'how's and 'when's, wanting it to happen in a certain way at a certain time. This is your ego's agenda and not your soul's journey. Remember, your ego pushes and rushes, while your soul trusts and flows.

Think of it like this: when you order a parcel, do you worry about how it will get to you and micromanage every step of the process? Do you call the company you've ordered it from straight away to make sure they have received the order, follow the fulfilment person around and tell them how to pack your order and then follow your package to the post room to make sure they post it in the way that you want them to? Do you get in the car with the delivery driver being a backseat driver and telling them how you'd like them to drive and which route to take? Do you follow them to your door telling them when and exactly how you'd like the package delivered?

I mean, you could, but how utterly exhausting and unnecessary would that be? So instead, you order something and trust that it will be delivered to you. You make sure that you know exactly what you want, order the right thing, put in the right address, make sure that you'll be home to receive it when it arrives and then you surrender the rest.

This is exactly what you need to do with your hopes, dreams, desires, intentions and manifestations. Get clear on what is alive within you wanting to be weaved and brought to life through you. Make your soul wishes, place your cosmic orders, let the universe know what you want and are ready for. Then do all that you can do to make these things happen – put yourself out there, take inspired action, work on yourself, push beyond any doubts and fears and clear up your side of the road making sure that you're all ready and prepared to receive it when it arrives.

Then surrender the rest and know it's coming – just like the metaphoric package I mentioned above. Don't worry about the 'how's and 'what's and 'when's. That's not for you to worry about, that's the universe's job and where the surrender, trust and patience come in. Pay attention to any doubts and fears that arise and, in these moments, deepen into more faith and connection with the universe, and trust that it's all coming in the perfect time.

One powerful way to do this is to begin to live like what you want is already here. If you already had what it is that you want, how would you act, behave and show up? This is how you begin to live in trust and energetic alignment with what you want – you start to live like it's already here as you have no doubt that the universe will deliver in perfect timing.

Living in this way, you get to take conscious control over your own cosmic purpose and become a powerful co-creator with the universe. You get to become an active participant in the unfolding of your soul's journey and allow your soul to weave, experience, create and live through you. You meet the universe halfway and then you surrender the rest. Know that the universe has heard you, your soul has a plan and, as long as you have done all that you can, this or something better is coming your way. Sink into deep trust and surrender knowing that you are always being supported and guided and have an entire cosmic realm on your side that wants the best for you and your soul's evolution.

You know what it truly means now to meet the universe halfway and have started to remove some blocks and fears. From here, we'll learn about your vibration and how to raise it.

WHISPERS FROM YOUR SOUL

- How do you need to begin to meet the universe halfway in creating the life that you desire?
- Why do you not believe that the universe will meet you halfway? What are your biggest block, doubts and fears around your manifestations?
- If you already had what you want, how would that change your life and how would you show up in the world? How can you begin to live like what you want is already here?

‘You attract abundance, joy and happiness into your life easily and effortlessly by simply making yourself a vibrational match for all that you want.’

Chapter 16

RAISE YOUR VIBRATION

I've mentioned a few times in this book that everything in the world is energy and vibrates at a certain frequency; this includes you, your body, your thoughts, your words, your actions and also your soul. When we are stuck in the doubts, fears and approval-seeking of our ego, we tend to vibrate at a lower frequency, and this takes us out of alignment with our soul frequency and therefore who our soul intends us to be.

You can't possibly evolve into the greatest, most soulful version of you when you are filling yourself and your life with things that aren't in alignment with what you want to manifest in your life and who you want to be. Part of your cosmic purpose is to raise your vibration and let go of all that keeps you out of alignment with that.

When you begin to walk a spiritual path, things in your life will begin to fall away – it's a hard yet inevitable truth about raising your vibration and moving into new levels of consciousness. Things you used to enjoy doing won't hold the same joy anymore; people you used to spend time with won't resonate with you anymore; ways you used to behave won't serve you anymore; beliefs you used to hold won't feel as true anymore – and there comes a point when you need to allow parts of you and your old life to fall away.

This begins with noticing your vibes: what makes you feel good, happy and positive, and what makes you feel low or flat and brings you down? As you begin to vibrate at more of your soul's frequency, you'll be able to notice what takes you out of alignment with that, and these are the things that need detoxing from your life.

The law of attraction says that like attracts like and whatever we are giving our energy, focus and attention to will multiply. Whatever energetic vibration you are sending out into the universe is what will come back to you amplified.

Have you ever had one of those days where you get out of bed on the wrong side and just feel irritable and out of sorts or start your day feeling angry at the world and everything – and I mean everything – seems to go wrong? It's the one day that you burn your toast and drop toothpaste down your top and there is a huge traffic jam and your boss shouts at you, and the shop or cafe doesn't have what you want for lunch, and it feels like the whole world is against you.

This is how the law of attraction and vibrations work – you get back more of what you give out, and the more you can begin to raise your vibration to the frequency of your soul, the more all that is meant for you will begin to easily come to you and all that is not in alignment with your soul self will begin to effortlessly fall away.

I want to stress here that this does not mean that we want to simply 'high vibe' ourselves all the time and spiritually bypass what we are feeling. Neither does it mean that if you have one bad thought, day, week or even month, you will ruin your whole life – that's not the way this works.

If you've followed me for long enough, you'll know that I very often speak on the fact that we gain many of our biggest breakthroughs in the so-called lower vibration emotions as, very often, it's only when we feel these that we really begin to pay attention and listen.

What we don't want to do is get stuck in these vibrations as this is when we will get completely out of alignment from our soul and our cosmic purpose, and begin to feel purposeless, unhappy, flat, low and hopeless. We want to stay long enough to learn the lesson and then raise our vibration to one that's more suited to where we want to be.

Shifting Your Energy

Begin with yourself and notice what thoughts, beliefs and stories you are holding on to that are bringing down your vibe and keeping you operating on a lower level. Things like fear, shame, judgement, guilt, hatred, anger and resentment vibrate at a lower frequency and will keep you trapped in loops, attracting similar energy into your life.

The more you can become aware of your emotional state and begin to shift your vibration, the more quickly and easily you'll begin to manage your own inner frequency and allow yourself to vibrate at the energy of your soul rather than getting mindlessly caught in the doubts and fears of your ego or the outside world.

Begin to notice over the coming days how things feel in your body and energy:

- ❍ Do you feel drained after spending time with certain people, in certain situations or after doing certain things?
- ❍ What are you consuming through the media and social media, and how is that making you feel?

- What are you eating, drinking, watching, listening to and consuming in general and how does that make you feel?

Notice who or what knocks you off centre, makes you doubt yourself or your dreams, doesn't support your growth, makes you feel less than or tries to pull you away from what you want or back into old versions of you or patterns or behaviours.

Look at where you are holding on to anger, resentments and the past – this is a sure-fire way to keep yourself stuck in low vibration energy that pulls you from your soul path and cosmic purpose. Pay attention to where you are leaking your energy by comparing yourself to someone else or giving away your power to others.

Look at your life and be honest about where you are out of alignment, off track, being someone you're not and giving your energy to things that don't serve you. Pay real attention to what depletes and steals your energy, and begin to do less of that and more of what nourishes you, lights and fills you up, and makes you feel good. This simple act in itself will help you to begin to move more consciously towards your cosmic purpose.

Learn to protect your vibration and walk away from things that drain your soul, and set boundaries around things that make you feel like less of yourself. Be willing to sacrifice what is not aligned with your soul purpose and takes you off your path. Don't give your precious time and energy to things that don't make you feel good – choose what honours your energy.

Begin to vibrate at the frequency of who you want to be. When you vibrate at the frequency of someone who is strong and powerful, knows their worth and who they are, and isn't afraid to speak their truth, you will no longer attract people who don't know your worth or situations that don't value or honour you.

As you begin to shift your inner frequency, your outer reality will begin to shift too. As you align with the energy of your soul, all that is a vibrational match and meant for you will begin to come to you and you will start to be in the right place at the right time, meet the right people, receive the right messages, know instinctively and intuitively what to do next and begin to allow your soul to experience life through you.

You will start to live at the frequency of your soul self, and this is where miracles occur – you think of someone, and they call; you need something, and it arrives. You attract abundance, joy, happiness, love and all that you desire into your life easily and effortlessly by simply making yourself a vibrational match for all that you want.

Find pockets of gratitude, love, joy, happiness and appreciation everywhere you can and, when you find them, *feel* them with every part of your being. Sit in the vibration of your soul as often as you can, and *feel* this in every cell of your being. Raise your vibration as quickly as you can, and *feel* the vibration of what it is that you do want to experience, and your life will begin to change instantly. And from this place of being in your highest soul's vibration, you can more easily trust the process, as we'll explore now.

WHISPERS FROM YOUR SOUL

- Do you tend to live in the lower or higher states of vibration?
- How can you begin to raise your vibration on a daily basis?
- What does it feel like to be in the vibration of your soul?

‘The simple act of acceptance for what you are going through, even if you don’t like or understand it, will bring an almost immediate peace and align you back with your soul.’

Chapter 17

TRUST THE PROCESS

It's easy to be spiritual when it's all going well and life is going your way, but do you trust in the universe, life and your soul in the moments when it isn't? One of the key parts of beginning to live a life of cosmic purpose is trusting the process of how your life is unfolding. This can feel incredibly difficult to begin with, but, as you learn to trust you, your soul, life and the universe even more, this is when life begins to get really exciting, and you start to live in the flow of your soul and fulfil more of what you came here to do.

There are going to be moments on the spiritual journey when you lose your faith, you get tested and it feels like everything is falling apart, life is against you and nothing is working the way you want it to – I like to call these spiritual stumbles.

It's inevitable that you will face difficulties as you walk this path, as part of your journey is overcoming challenges and learning the lessons that your soul needs you to learn in this lifetime to grow and evolve into the most soulful version of you. It's how you choose to face these challenges that will make all the difference to your journey.

If you could begin to embrace the hard, sad and difficult times in the same way that you embrace the happy, joyful and fun times – the times when it's all flowing and working out – your life would change in an instant.

What usually causes the most amount of suffering in the more difficult moments in life is not the situation itself, but your perception of it and the story that your ego tells you about what is happening. You believe it shouldn't be happening the way it is, you judge it and fight against it, and this makes it all feel so much worse and out of your control.

Your ego tries to grip, control, manipulate, cajole and change what is happening to fit its narrative of what it wants. But the more this happens, the further you get from your soul path and what your soul currently wants to experience through you. The harder life then gets and the more you feel disconnected from your soul and your purpose. In times like this it's so vital to remember that this is happening *for* you not *to* you.

Very often, when little human us is micromanaging over here getting all anxious, upset and stressed, when life doesn't seem to be going our way, the universe has something way better over there for us that we are missing by continuing to gaze at a door that should have long been closed or trying to force something that isn't for us.

Life is always working for you, even in the moments when it feels like it isn't. Everything that you are experiencing, especially the harder and more challenging times, are to help you to grow and deepen your faith and trust, and redirect you on to your soul path and into your purpose.

Surrendering to Your Soul

Are you only able to trust the universe and your soul when things are all working out? That's not real faith. Real faith is when you can dig deep and find trust when nothing at all makes sense, and it seems to all be falling apart. This is when you surrender to your soul and truly begin to trust that life is always working for you and trying to move you towards your cosmic purpose.

In moments when I am finding life hard or challenging, I remind myself that my soul has chosen this for me, and my soul wouldn't choose anything that I couldn't get through. This brings me so much comfort and helps me to lean into the part of me who knows – the soul part of me who knows that what I am going through is teaching me something and helping me to evolve in some way or realise more of who I am (or am not).

As we've already touched on, it may feel confronting to believe that you/your soul has chosen many of the difficult, hard and traumatic times in your life, and there may be a big part of you that wants to reject that and continue to believe that it's someone or something else's fault that your life is the way it is or that life just isn't fair. While this may initially feel like an easier thought and belief, it's really disempowering. You are giving the whole experience of your life away to something outside of you and then have to wait for that person or situation to change before you can be happy, which you may be waiting a lifetime for.

When you can begin to believe that your soul has chosen this for you, you take back the power over your own life. It becomes your experience and your lesson, and you begin to manoeuvre through these experiences differently. You are no longer waiting for something or someone in the outside world to change. Instead, you can now begin to look for the lesson and the gift in what you are going through and the changes that you need to make within.

Rather than feeling like a victim to circumstance or life, you get to allow this experience to teach you, alchemise you, break you down and crack you wide open. Ask yourself:

- 'How can I experience more of my soul through this time?'
- 'What is this showing me and teaching me about me and my life?'
- 'Where am I being called to love myself more, honour myself more, choose myself more, put myself out there more or let go of a version of me or something in my life?'

Notice where you are stuck in trying to have it all figured out or get the answers or going into worst-case scenarios or what could go wrong, and let all of that go. When you struggle and fight against what is, you block the flow of what wants to make its way to you. Shift your focus into a space of deep trust, surrender and knowing that you are always being guided.

Imagine if you were able to see everything that happens to you as a lesson from your soul to help you to evolve into all that your soul knows you can be. Imagine if, rather than crumbling and going into fear and frustration, you were able to call on your soul for help and guidance: 'I know this is happening for me, not to me. Please help me to get through this. Please show me what I need to know. Please bring me the wisdom, strength and guidance that I need.'

When you begin to trust the process, everything changes and you can flow with life, surrendering to what is rather than fighting against it. The simple act of acceptance for what you are going through, even if you don't like or understand it, will bring an almost immediate peace as it takes you out of your ego and aligns you back with your soul.

Your ego will always think it knows best about what needs to happen in life, but what if life is working for you in these moments when you feel like it isn't? What if that rejection is a redirection to something even better? What if the door isn't opening as it's not your door or there is nothing behind it for you? What if it's all crumbling as you're holding on to things not meant for you and the universe needs you to allow these things to fall away? What if this test of faith is deepening your faith? What if this hard time is asking you to go deep within and realise how strong, powerful and resilient you are?

Sometimes you need to fall so that who you are becoming can catch you. Sometimes when it's falling apart it's actually coming together. In those moments when you are not getting what you want, it's because the universe has something even better waiting for you. We sometimes only see this after the event – sometime in the future when we can connect the dots and it all makes more sense. But part of the journey is in being able to find the trust even in the moments when it doesn't all seem to be working out.

What you'll come to see as you discover your cosmic purpose is that every struggle you go through in life is an initiation into something greater – it's moulding you into a more expanded, limitless version of you. It's helping to show you the stuck, afraid parts of you who still exist within you and the parts of you who still need healing, holding and releasing. Like the phoenix from the flames, these difficult times in your life are helping to burn it all to the ground so that you can emerge from the ashes.

It's likely that what you are going through right now is preparing you for what you have been asking for. Remember that your soul has a divine plan for you and it's in the unfolding of the journey that you will learn all that you need to be able to hold all that is waiting for you when it's time to receive it.

Trust that a part of you knows just what all of this is for, allow the process and surrender to your soul. This is an evolution, an awakening, a preparation. The more you can surrender to what is and not try to fight it, the more life can weave through you and bring through the solutions, answers and direction.

Especially if something you are going after is a soul calling, it's likely there will be obstacles and hard times along the way as it's all helping you to grow into your full potential. As I've touched on throughout this book, there is a common misconception that, when you're going after a soul dream, things will just be easy and perfect and fall effortlessly into place and, if they don't, it means it's not meant to be. This couldn't be further from the truth.

Yes, the universe will guide, help and support you, but it will also bring little challenges along the way to perhaps test how much you truly want it and what you're willing to do to get there. How much do you truly want something if you give up at the first sign of it being hard? If you can't handle a small knockback, rejection or problem on the road to what you want, what hope do you have of being able to hold it when it arrives? What you face along the way of getting to your dream is helping you to grow into the version of you who can hold that dream when you get there.

If all that you want came too easily, you wouldn't appreciate it and would likely sabotage it when you got it as a part of not feeling worthy of it. When you have had to go through challenges and difficulties and really dig deep into yourself to get something, you can own it when it arrives. You can stand proud in the knowledge that you did that, you achieved that, you created that and you made that happen. You faced so many challenges to get there and you never gave up. Even in the hard times, you held the faith and made it happen. This helps you to trust and believe in yourself more so that you can begin to go after even bigger and better things.

When you can lean into the trust that you are always being supported and guided and trust the process, even in the difficult and more challenging times, your life will change and, rather than struggle, you can surrender into the support of your soul. Human you may have no idea what is going on, but soul you does – trust that and surrender to a higher source of power, which we'll explore in the next chapter.

WHISPERS FROM YOUR SOUL

- If you were to allow yourself to believe that everything you go through in life is part of your soul purpose, how would that change the way you see your life, especially the hard times?
- Can you look back at a time in your life when you felt it was all going wrong and now see that it was all working out perfectly and in your favour?
- In what areas of your life do you find it hardest to trust the process and why?

‘The universe always has a plan and, in surrender, you allow that plan to unfold.’

Chapter 18

SURRENDER TO A HIGHER SOURCE OF POWER

Not only do you have the entire universe on your side, but there is also a part of you that always knows just what you are going through and why, as well as what it is taking you towards. You do not have to struggle through life and do it all alone; at any time, you can surrender it all up to a higher power and receive grace, help and guidance from your higher self, soul and the universe.

Frequently, little human you thinks they know best – I very often have to smile at little human me as she thinks she knows better than the entire universe about the way things should be. Our ego wants things to work out in the exact way that it wants it to. And when things don't quite work out in this way, our ego gets upset and life suddenly feels like a scary and confusing place that makes us feel uncertain and afraid.

There are going to be times when life makes no sense to human you. It's all part of the journey and helping you to not only deepen into more trust, but also to remember the incredible support that you have available to you at all times. The more we try to figure it out all alone, the further we move from our soul selves and the guidance of the universe and the more alone we feel.

Trusting in the Divine

In moments when you feel alone, lost, confused, uncertain or afraid, or when life feels like it's falling apart, don't struggle; give it up to something greater than you. Say to the higher part of you, to the universe: 'I don't know what to do right now, please help me.' This simple act will surrender it all to a higher power and allow this energy to come into your life and help guide you.

When you are gripping too tightly and trying to control things or needing a certain outcome, which our ego often does out of fear, you strangle the flow of support, guidance and all that wants to come through to you. You are resisting the natural flow of life and not allowing life to be lived through you. You can't see the solutions, hear the answers or see the bigger picture, and this is when things get even more confusing and uncertain.

As soon as you let go of control and surrender, you invite the higher, wiser parts of you to come in and figure it all out for you. This is when you can begin to allow life to organise itself around you, allowing all that needs to fall away to fall away and everything else to land where it needs to be.

This helps you to get out of your own way and allow universal guidance and wisdom to come in. It brings answers where you'd only had questions, solutions where you'd only had problems, an opening where you'd only seen a dead end and an alternative route where you'd only thought there was one way to go.

In difficult and challenging times, don't give up. Instead, give up everything that you are struggling with – all that feels heavy and difficult and impossible and heartbreaking – to a higher power. Trust that you are always being supported and guided, and allow this higher power to hold you and show you the way forward.

Surrender the struggle, surrender the suffering and with this will come a sense of deep trust and peace as you open up to solutions and possibilities that are way beyond your human understanding. The universe always has a plan and, in surrender, you allow it to unfold.

I also like to apply this same method when I'm manifesting or calling something into my life. When setting intentions, visualising or asking for what I want, I always ask 'for this or something better'. This means that I don't limit what wants to come to me through the conditioning and expectations of my ego mind. It opens up the space for something more magical and wonderful than I had ever imagined coming to me, perhaps in a different way than I had expected it to. It helps me to surrender my dreams and desires to a higher source of power and create from the expansion of my soul rather than the restrictions of my mind.

Very often, human you will only dream half a dream for fear that it's not going to come true or because it fears that you may not actually be able to make it happen. You worry about how you're going to make it happen or all that could go wrong. And your ego mind gets caught up in what it wants and expects, and that what you want can only come in a certain way at a certain time under a certain set of conditions. This restricts the flow of all that wants to make its way to you.

As soon as you ask for 'this or something better', as soon as you surrender your manifestations to a higher power, you open yourself to the flow of your soul and allow your soul to weave its magic through you and bring what wants to be brought into your life, often in even better ways than you had imagined.

I also ask for it to be for my higher good and the highest good of all. This ensures that, through bringing to life what wants to be brought to life through me and becoming all of who I came here to be, I get to touch the lives of those I am meant to and make a difference to the world in ways I am perhaps not even aware of. It allows me to expand into higher consciousness and make the impossible possible by allowing my soul self to guide the way.

When you begin to trust in a higher power that is guiding you and surrender to that, your life will change in so many ways. Know that you have divine, universal energy flowing through you and, as soon as you give up your ego's plan in favour of the divine plan, this energy can flow through you and guide you to where you need to be. This helps you to trust in the divine timing of life, which we'll dive into now.

WHISPERS FROM YOUR SOUL

- Where is your human plan getting in the way of the divine plan?
- What are you currently struggling with and how can you surrender it to a higher power?
- What areas of life do you struggle with most and try to control, grip and micromanage or feel like you have to figure it out all alone?

‘When you understand that there is always a greater guiding force taking care of you, you can allow your cosmic purpose to unfold without rushing it and enjoy the journey.’

Chapter 19

TRUST THE TIMING

I joke about this a lot, but we live in a world where we want to Amazon Prime our entire lives. We want to do one meditation and be enlightened; one yoga class and be able to do a handstand; one moon ritual and change our entire lives. We want everything immediately, right now, and try to push and rush and make life adhere to our next-day delivery schedule.

But that's not quite the way that life works and, very often, the universe has a way better plan than the speedy fast-track one that your ego wants to make happen. This is where we need to learn to trust the timing of life, of our soul's journey and of all that is coming to us in perfect timing and often in even better ways than we imagined.

I learned this lesson so beautifully in my journey of going to India to become a yoga teacher. As I shared in the Introduction, it took me nearly two years to make this dream happen and these were some of the most difficult, challenging and yet, with hindsight, most profound and life-changing years of my life.

I'd discovered yoga and wanted to follow my dream to India, to where yoga came from, and fully immerse myself in the practice and teachings. Yet, I was working in a corporate job and, without a huge amount of savings behind me, I wasn't sure how I would make it happen. I'd lock myself in the toilet every day at work and cry my eyes out. I'd plead to the universe that I wanted to do something that would truly help others and why wouldn't the universe just help me to do that. In those times, I used to debate whether it was more painful to have no dream at all or a dream that was so alive yet wasn't coming true.

But, as distant and difficult as it felt, that dream of going to India just wouldn't go away. The corporate world became more of a challenge to be in – I just didn't relate to so much of it and I was being horribly treated by an awful colleague. I couldn't understand why the universe was making me stay there when I was so deeply unhappy. I handed in my notice three times, and each time got a promotion and pay rise, which helped me to start to save the money to be able to go to India.

I decided one day that, rather than suffer my way through where I was in life, I'd start to see it as a game, like soul school, and I'd trust that everything that was happening was helping to get me to where I wanted to be. I got curious about what the bullying from the colleague was bringing up in me and how I could choose to respond rather than react to the situation. I looked at where my woundings were and how I was allowing certain behaviours.

I deepened my craft, diving into my yoga practice and studies, learning as much as I could. I got clear on my dream of going to India and trusted not only in the universe, but also in myself to make it happen. I created a vision board on my desk at work, with images of India and yoga all over it that I looked at every day. I leaned into the trust that it was going to happen. I didn't know how or when, but I knew that it would.

Sure enough, two years later, it did. On my final day at work, everyone looked at me like I was slightly crazy, but I know deep down that so many of them wished they were brave enough to do what I was doing. In fact, I've had quite a few messages over the years from people I worked with back then to say that I inspired them to be brave enough to follow a dream of their own, and that makes me so happy.

I share this part of my journey not only to speak of the timing and how there is always a bigger plan in place for you, but also to encourage you that you too can do this – you can follow a big dream and make it happen. I'm no one special; I was just a girl with a big dream that I could not give up on, even though there were times when it felt like it was never going to happen. Trust in your dreams and, most of all, trust in the timing of them coming true.

As much as those few years were testing, and at times it felt like I would never be able to make my dream come true, I know now that had I gone to India one year, one month or even one week sooner than I did, I would not be sitting here writing these words to you now. I wasn't ready to go any sooner. There were still things I needed to learn, ways I needed to grow and evolve and get to know myself, and my soul knew that. Those years were preparing me for the journey when it was the right time.

I could so easily have given up on that dream, decided it was too hard or wasn't happening quickly enough, but there was an intuitive nudge, an inner knowing that was so certain that this was my path that I just couldn't give it up, no matter how hard it felt. I had to hold the trust and belief that I would somehow make it happen. I'm so happy that I trusted the timing and allowed it to all happen as it was meant to.

My story of timing and trust doesn't end there. I finally got to India – the dream – and spent every day for the first week crying my eyes out wanting to go home. Travelling in India alone as a woman is tough. I had this fantasy that I'd get to India and everything would unfold so perfectly, and it didn't. I'd call home and have to pretend it was a bad line and put the phone down as I was crying so hard. I wanted to be able to share stories of how utterly wonderful and magical and spiritual it was and how I'd reached enlightenment already. But if someone had offered me a plane ticket home in that first week I think I'd have been tempted to take it.

Once again, the universe and my soul knew best. This time it taught me the most about myself I think I have ever learned. I learned to trust myself, rely on myself and really love myself. In moments of feeling alone and afraid, I'd put my cheek against my naked shoulder feeling skin to skin and hold myself and say, 'It's ok Kirst, I've got you, I'm not going anywhere.' I'd make little deals with myself about going to the end of the street and then I could come back or being brave enough to go visit a certain place. I found my inner strength and resilience, and came to know that I was always there with me and would look after me.

The timing of all of it was perfect, just as it was meant to be, even if it wasn't how human me envisaged it.

Surrendering to the Flow

When you begin to understand that there is always a greater guiding force taking care of you, you can begin to allow your cosmic purpose to unfold without rushing it and enjoy the journey.

When you are rushing and pushing your life, you can be sure that your ego is in control. Your soul knows that everything is in perfect timing. You are right where you need to be, right now. If this wasn't where you were meant to be, you wouldn't be here – you'd be somewhere different. In the same way all that happened in your past happened the way it was supposed to, if it was meant to have happened any other way it would have. Everything in your life is unfolding in just the way that it's meant to and, very often, the only thing in the way of that is you. Your ego wants it in a different way, in a different time, while your soul is whispering to just trust.

Just because it feels like something is not working out the way that your ego wants it to it, it doesn't mean that's it's not all working out perfectly. Maybe you aren't quite ready yet and would sabotage what you say you want if it came to you right now. Maybe there are pieces of the puzzle that need to fall into place that you can't quite see or understand, but the universe is working behind the scenes to make it all happen for you. Maybe the universe knows that you are worthy and deserve more than you are currently asking for and is waiting for you to also realise that so it can give you something way better.

Perhaps that job you didn't get is because there is an even better one out there for you, and the universe is waiting for the person currently in the role to hand in their notice or for you to expand into the version of you who can step into that role. Perhaps that relationship didn't work out as there is someone else out there who is even more aligned with your soul who will give you more of what you need or it's in this break-up and heartbreak that you will learn to love yourself and become a truer, more authentic version of you.

Very often, when something is taking its time to get to you, it's because there is something even better coming your way, or you are being moulded and prepared so that you can hold what you want when it arrives. Nothing meant for you will ever pass you by; trust that. You do, of course, need to meet the universe halfway, which we explored in Chapter 15, but then surrender it all, trust in the timing and enjoy the unfolding of your cosmic purpose.

One of the best ways that you can do this is to practise

acceptance. This doesn't mean that you have to like where you currently are in your life or that what you want isn't here yet, but with acceptance comes surrender. Rather than fighting with life, you can flow with it and align with your soul's plan. You cannot control divine timing; that's the universe's job. What you can control are your thoughts, vibrations, behaviours and what you do with your time and life while you are waiting.

Rather than berating the fact that what you want isn't here yet, feel into how you can use this time to learn, grow, expand and be ready for what you want when it arrives. Learn from what you are experiencing in your life right now and what this is teaching and showing you. See this current time in your life as part of the assignment that is taking you towards where you want to go. Don't put your life on hold waiting and wishing – do what you can do to get you to where you need to be and trust that all that you want, and perhaps even better, is making its way to you in perfect timing when you are ready.

You also need to practise non-attachment. This means being committed to what you want and then letting go of the how, and especially the when, and trying to force your ego's timeframe on your life. All you need to do is hold the vision and trust that the universe has a planning department that knows just when you are ready, and the time is right.

Stop trying to push open doors that aren't opening for you and instead know that doors are going to open for you when you are ready – and often with something even better behind them than you had ever hoped or wished for. Relax into the knowing that the universe is taking care of you, and everything is always working in your favour in the perfect timing if you just allow it.

One thing that will really help you to trust the timing is to lean on your spiritual support squad. Let's meet them now . . .

WHISPERS FROM YOUR SOUL

- ❍ Looking back over your life, can you see times when you so desperately wanted something to happen, but, with hindsight, you can see there was a reason it didn't as there was something better waiting for you or it wasn't the right time?
- ❍ Where are you trying to rush and push and Amazon Prime your journey, allowing your ego to take over and think it knows best rather than trusting in the timing of your soul?
- ❍ If something that you are dreaming about hasn't quite come into your life just yet, what could this time be teaching you or how are you being called to prepare for what you want when it arrives?

‘Your spiritual support squad holds the map of your journey and can assist you when you get lost, confused or forget your way.’

Chapter 20

LEAN ON YOUR SPIRITUAL SUPPORT SQUAD

One of the most amazing things about this journey is that you don't need to do it alone. You have an entire team, a spiritual support squad, just waiting to help you when you ask.

And that's one of the most important things you need to learn on this journey – you need to ask for help when you need it. As you have free will as a human, your guides, angels, ancestors and ascended masters cannot intervene (unless it's a life-threatening emergency that happens before your chosen time to leave your body) and so you need to call on them for help and assistance, which they will be more than happy to provide. You can do this through meditation, prayer or just asking 'please help me' and feel the rush of support that comes in to hold and guide you.

Let's look at some of the support available to you . . .

Your Spirit Guide

Each one of us comes to earth with a spirit guide whose role it is to support you in reaching your soul's full potential and accomplish all that you came here to learn in this lifetime. You may remember that in Chapter 3 I shared with you that you decide on your life lessons with your guide, and they hold this map of your journey and can assist you when you get lost, confused or forget your way.

Your spirit guide loves and supports you unconditionally (even when you are straying in the wrong direction or ignoring them!) and provides a source of guidance, inspiration, comfort and wisdom. They will help you to navigate challenges, make more sense of confusing situations and support you in moments of doubt and fear. They will also encourage and guide you, and sometimes even gently (or not so gently!) nudge you towards more of your cosmic purpose.

Your spirit guide knows all of who you are and all of who you can be. They know all of who you've been and all that you will ever be. They know soul you, and want to help you to remember that version of you and complete your soul lessons in this lifetime.

Unlike angels or archangels, who we'll meet in just a moment, your spirit guide was most likely once human, just like you, and understands the human journey and struggles. They have themselves been through many incarnations and learned all of what it is to be human, and now choose to remain in the spiritual realms and guide others on their human experience.

Getting to know your spirit guide is a beautiful journey towards uncovering more of your cosmic purpose. To begin with, start communicating with your guide asking for signs and their help and assistance in moments when you feel lost, confused or afraid. Talk to your guide like you would with a best friend; ask for their advice or support and tell them of your struggles.

You can also meet your spirit guide in meditation asking them to make themselves known to you. You might ask their name and for them to give you a sign that tells you when they are close by. You may be able to see or feel them with you and, over time, begin to hear their voice as they guide and support you.

Just a little word on this: when you initially hear the voice of your guide, it may be disappointing, and you may doubt it as it sounds kind of like your own. I remember when I first started working with my spirit guide I expected their voice to come from somewhere outside of me, perhaps like that old lottery advert where the voice boomed 'It could be you' from the sky.

Yet the voice of my guide sounded like mine and, for a long time, I doubted that it could be true. I now believe that our guides initially do this to help us feel safer and more comfortable as we open the communication channels. The more you work with your guide, the more you will notice they use words that you wouldn't or a tone of voice that's slightly different to your own and, over time, you will learn to recognise their voice as very distinct and different to yours.

You will also learn their personality and ways and, just be warned, most spirit guides have a wonderful sense of humour – I guess they feel that as part of this human experience you just have to laugh!

You can also call on your spirit guide to help you when you are finding things difficult with other people. When you are both in your egos and struggling to find a solution or make peace with someone, you can ask your guide to talk to their guide and find a spiritual solution – trust me on this, just try it; you'll be amazed at the results.

Helper guides

Alongside your spirit guide, you may also have helper guides who come in to assist you with different areas of your life. These may be abundance guides, relationship guides, healing guides or teacher guides. Each one of these will come in to support you with something more specific and help you to learn and evolve in different ways.

You may choose these guides by asking for assistance in certain areas of your life or they may choose you, dropping in alongside your spirit guide to bring extra support and guidance. These guides may come in for just a short time or stay with you for years or a lifetime if you have deeper work to do together. You can communicate with helper guides in the same way as you do with your spirit guide.

Guardian Angels

As well as a spirit guide, we all also have a guardian angel who remains with us our whole lives and is there to protect and guide us on our journey. Whereas your spirit guide has lived a human experience, your guardian angel hasn't and is of the highest and purest vibration.

You can connect to your guardian angel in the same way as your spirit guide and you will often feel them as a warm, loving, supportive presence that surrounds you with unconditional love. Pray to your guardian angel, ask for their help, assistance, support and guidance, and feel them close by you at all times, but especially in times of need and difficulty.

Archangels

Archangels are divine spiritual beings and messengers who are here to support in the future of humanity. They will work with whoever asks and has need of them, and they possess great power and authority, helping us to raise our awareness and strengthen our connection with the universe. It is uncertain just how many archangels there are, but here are some of the main ones:

- **Archangel Michael:** known as the warrior of light, he is the great protector and most powerful of the archangels. Call upon Michael when you need protection or to remove negative energy from your life. He is associated with blue light or seeing flashes of light.
- **Archangel Raphael:** the divine healer, Raphael will help you to heal your body, mind, heart and spirit. He guides you towards inner harmony and coming back into balance with your soul self. Call upon him when you need healing in any form. He is associated with emerald green light or hearing whispers, especially in nature.
- **Archangel Gabriel:** the heavenly messenger Gabriel will help you to communicate with the universe, your higher self and understand your own inner wisdom. He will also help you to communicate with others, finding the right words to say and assist you with writing and other creative projects. He is associated with yellow or peace lilies.
- **Archangel Chamuel:** the archangel of peace and unconditional love, Chamuel will help you in times when you feel lost or alone or when you are struggling to love yourself. Call

on him to know that you are love and loved, especially in moments of doubt and anxiety, and feel the vibration of love in and around you. He also assists with relationships. He is associated with pink and seeing hearts and roses.

- **Archangel Zadkiel:** the archangel of transmutation, Zadkiel helps you to move through challenging energy and emotions, and alchemise them into divine wisdom and growth. He helps with forgiveness and fear, and releasing the past, painful memories and stuck emotions. Call on him when you are resisting life and need to surrender. He is associated with purple, butterflies and lavender flowers.
- **Archangel Azrael:** the archangel of grief, Azrael brings comfort and support in times of deep loss and grieving. He supports souls in transitioning from human form back into the spiritual, and surrounds those in mourning with gentle, loving support, bringing healing through the grieving process. Call on him when your heart is breaking and feel his strength and guidance. He is associated with white light and seeing feathers to show you that loved ones are nearby.
- **Archangel Metatron:** one of only two archangels who experienced a human incarnation and ascended to an archangel, Metatron helps us too to ascend, transform and remember our spiritual power. He is the keeper of the 'akashic records' (we'll discuss these in more detail in the next chapter) and will help you to understand your journey in this lifetime, assisting you in releasing what is not serving you and raising your vibrational frequency. He is associated with orange or flashes of sunset-like light and seeing repeating numbers, especially 11 and 12.

Earth Angels

Every now and then, we will come across someone on the earthly plane who we know is here to guide, protect, support or assist us in some way – these are known as earth angels. These high vibrational beings from the spiritual realms and the cosmos choose to incarnate as humans walking the earth alongside us to assist us in raising the vibration of earth.

You may come across an earth angel in a passing moment, but they change the course of your life forever, or you may be lucky enough to have them walk alongside you for a little longer or guide you from afar.

You will know when you meet an earth angel. They will come to you at just the right moment and give you just what you need. They will guide and support you and your life will change in some way after being in their presence.

Bear in mind that you may be an earth angel, so pay attention to where you can give a smile to a stranger in the moment they need it or do a kindness for someone that seems like something so small to you, but changes their life in a meaningful way, which you may never realise.

Ascended Masters

Ascended masters are beings of love and light who once lived (many lifetimes) as humans and gained self-mastery, reached enlightenment and have now ascended so no longer need to reincarnate, but choose to guide our collective consciousness.

They are beings such as Jesus, Mary Magdalene, St Germain, Lady Nada, Lord Maitreya, Grandmother Anna, Lord Melchizedek, and so many more. You can call upon these wise teachers for support and guidance, and to teach you more about your human experience. They can also help you to begin to vibrate at a higher frequency more in alignment with your soul self.

Ancestors and Loved Ones

Ancestors and loved ones who have passed over are always with you. Call upon your loved ones and ancestors and feel their loving presence with you. Talk to them like they are still here, right by your side, which they are; they are just beyond the veil. Feel them like guardians protecting, guiding and supporting you. Hear their voice as they whisper to you or give you signs to let you know they are still with you.

From meeting your spiritual support squad, let's dive a little deeper into the journey now and explore your soul contracts, past lives and the akashic records.

WHISPERS FROM YOUR SOUL

- ❍ Who in your spiritual support squad are you most called to work with right now? Trust your initial vibes. I remember when I first started working with guides and angels and would feel like I needed to try to work with them all and that they would be upset if I worked with others and not them – they won't be! Don't rush the process. Start slowly and build upon this communication and, most of all, enjoy the journey to getting to know your team. You have so much support surrounding you; it's time to lean into it.
- ❍ What assistance do you want from your support squad right now? What do you need them to help you with?
- ❍ How are your support squad making themselves known to you? Do you feel, see, sense or hear them?

‘Part of the journey of your soul through multiple lifetimes is to complete soul contracts, which are all housed in the akashic records.’

Chapter 21

EXPLORE YOUR SOUL CONTRACTS AND PAST LIVES

In this chapter, we will explore your soul contracts, past lives and the akashic records, as all of these weave together to help you to understand more about yourself and your cosmic purpose in this lifetime, which is often to heal, clear and complete contracts from this and past lifetimes.

We forget our past lives and soul contracts for a similar reason that we forget all about our soul connection when we come to earth, so that we can explore and discover them through our human existence and use them to learn, grow and evolve into more of our soul self.

Let's begin with soul contracts.

Soul Contracts

When we sit with our guides before we come to earth and decide on the lessons and experiences that we want to have in this lifetime, these are our soul contracts or agreements that we make with ourselves and others that guide our experiences, lessons and growth. They represent what we want to work through to help us achieve more of our life purpose.

As we've touched on in previous chapters, as a human, you have free will – your human journey is a game, not a fully scripted play – and so you can choose whether or not to fulfil or complete any of these contracts when you come to earth. This is why some of these soul contracts you will clear in a single lifetime, while others will be carried over multiple lifetimes. The more aware you can try to become of your contracts, the more quickly you can complete them.

Some of these contracts may still be held from past lives. For example, it's common to create vows of celibacy or poverty in past lives that get carried over if they are not cleared, and so if you find yourself perpetually unable to meet anyone or always struggling with finances it can be worth exploring your contracts and akashic records and revoking any vows that are no longer serving you. We'll look at how to do this a little later.

You may also have made contracts around needing to earn your worth or your right to exist or stepping into your power or being of service to others, and so you will face tests and challenges to encourage you to fulfil these contracts and complete what your soul came here to do.

Many of these contracts involve other people, agreeing that we will come into each other's lives for a reason to either support each other or learn a deep soul lesson together. For example, you may want to learn the art of forgiveness and so another soul will take on the responsibility of deeply hurting and betraying you so that you can learn to either forgive or stay resentful, close off your heart or become a victim. You may need to learn boundaries and to stand up for yourself, so your soul will call in a colleague or boss who will try to control or bully you. Or perhaps your soul wants to learn self-love and to choose yourself, and so another soul will agree to continually not choose you or abandon you so that you have to learn to love and choose yourself over them.

Usually, the deeper and more painful the lesson of the contract, the closer we are to that person on a soul level as we trust them to do this to us and go through with this lesson for our own highest good – which is why I also mentioned in Chapter 3 that this is why we often find it the hardest to let go of those people who really hurt us.

Although your soul may indeed recognise the soul within them, it's vitally important to honour the closing of contracts on a human level and the earth plane and not try to hold on to them, as this will prolong the pain and block the lessons and completion of contracts and your soul growth. You also cannot complete anyone else's contract for them, which is why it's important to just focus on your own growth and know that you fulfilled your end of the contract, even if they didn't.

Fulfilling your soul contracts helps you to contribute to your soul's ongoing journey through multiple lifetimes and fulfil more of your cosmic purpose. One way to begin to recognise your soul contracts is to notice what challenges and difficulties you seem to keep facing over and over again, as you are supposed to learn from them. If you keep ignoring or remaining unaware of these contracts, the lessons will get harder and harder until you face them. Look for themes and patterns that seem to keep recurring in your life.

Begin to look at what you think the contract may be – this can be a general theme of what always seems to play out in your life or where you most struggle, and doesn't need to be in any great detail to begin with. Then, look at the intention of this contract and what it is teaching you or how it's asking you to grow and evolve.

Many contracts will naturally close or release when you have completed them by learning the appropriate lessons and taking action, setting boundaries or making changes or new choices and decisions in your life. You will know this has happened when you stop feeling the same way about certain people or situations or no longer keep behaving in the same ways or seeing the same dynamics show up in your life.

There may also be times when you need to close a contract or ask for it to be released or updated. This is particularly true if you feel that you have learned your part in a relationship dynamic, but the other person keeps trying to come back into your life or you feel there are still some energetic attachments there. This can also be done if a current version of your relationship isn't working and needs to be completed for you to get to the next level.

To do this, call in your spirit guide (if you work with them – see page 152). Now, call in the guide of the other person – visualise the other person opposite you and see them from a soul perspective. Now, visualise your soul agreement between you and say: 'Thank you so much for this contract and the lessons and teachings. This contract is now complete. I let it go with love and gratitude.' See the contract going up in flames, being transmuted and alchemised. You may also send the other person love, release any cords or ties between you and see them float away surrounded by your love and gratitude for the lesson.

You can use a similar process for any contracts or past life vows that you have created for yourself. Either visualise this contract or write it down on a piece of paper. Give gratitude for this contract and how it has served you and state your willingness to now release it. Visualise it going up in flames, or you can safely set your paper alight and burn it, feeling the contract releasing.

If you are uncertain or confused about any contracts or are

finding them too challenging and would like them to be modified, ask your soul and the universe to intervene and help you to update any contracts in this lifetime. This doesn't mean that you won't still need to learn the lessons, but that perhaps the lessons can come in a slightly different way that helps you to understand and overcome them more easily from your human perspective.

There will also be times when you are given new soul contracts and assignments – these are usually in pivotal life or astrological moments where a shift of timeline becomes available, and you get to almost fast-track your soul's development. Or they may come at times when you know you've just completed a big contract by changing a behaviour or when you are having one of those beautiful moments when you realise, had that same thing happened a few months ago, you'd have reacted differently.

The new soul assignments may feel like an invitation to step into a new chapter, a new expansion and go beyond your comfort zone. You'll literally feel in every part of you that it's time to move into something new and different and align with more of your soul self. You may have an inkling of what the new assignment is or no idea at all, but whatever it is, say yes to your soul and follow it into a new adventure.

Working with your past lives can help you to understand more about your soul contracts, as very often we create contracts that will help us to clear, continue, learn or heal something from past lives. Let's look at these now . . .

Past Lives

I believe that I have lived many lifetimes before and will live many lifetimes again. I have been so fascinated by past lives that I became a regression therapist many years ago and have continually been awed by taking people through past life journeys to help them to understand more about themselves in this lifetime.

I remember taking one client through a profound journey where she was a Native American in a tragic time and gave me names, details and regrets of what had happened and the part she played. After this session, we researched what she had told me and discovered that this had all actually happened, down to every last detail. This was something that neither of us had any prior knowledge of (we had to dig deep to find the details – it's not an event that is well known in history). Although I fully believe in all of this, I was astounded by the truth and depth of her journey and what we uncovered. It cemented my belief in past lives and how they affect our current one.

I have knowledge of quite a few of my past lives. I have also been with current members of my family in past lives, yet in different relationship dynamics. Learning about these lifetimes has given me such a different understanding of our current relationships and why things are the way that they are in this lifetime. My past lives have also helped me to understand more of who I am in this lifetime and why, and where some of my issues and fears have come from, as well as how they have been repeated through lifetimes. This knowledge has also helped me to see how a past life version of me is still trying to keep me safe.

If you often repeat patterns that you can't seem to break, have particularly challenging relationships with close people in your life, experience irrational or unexplained fears and phobias or a recurrent lingering emotion that doesn't feel like yours, such as loneliness, this could all be linked to past lives. You may also visit places and feel like you've been there before, meet someone new who you know you've met before or feel a deep affinity for a particular time period, culture or country.

Exploring your past lives can enable you to access memories, experiences and contracts from past lifetimes and not only understand how they are affecting you in this lifetime, but also find resolutions and healing.

First, you need to feel into whether or not the idea of past lives feels true for you. If it does and something in your soul lights up at the thought of exploring your past lives, there are many ways that you can do this. One would be to go to a regression therapist and allow them to help you explore and work through past lives.

Another way to do this is with the help of your spirit guide or through meditation and visualisation. Ask your spirit guide to help you to access your past lives that are most meaningful for you right now or set an intention for your meditation that you want to explore your past lives. Create your safe space (see page 34 for guidance on how to do this), sit comfortably, close your eyes and take some time to breathe and centre yourself. Allow your awareness to go inwards and feel a sense of connecting to your soul self.

You may just remain in meditation for a set amount of time (set a timer) and allow insights and images about your past lives to come to you. You may even take a particular person or situation into your meditation with you and ask to explore anything relating to past lives. Keep a journal and pen next to you and note as much as you can remember after your meditation, even if it doesn't seem to make much sense at the time. You can also use visualisation and imagine walking along a corridor and choosing a doorway to enter, knowing that there will be a meaningful past life memory behind that door. It's important to trust what comes to you without trying to question or make logical sense of it; things will get easier the more you practice.

Over time, as you connect more to your soul and build trust, you will begin to access your past life memories much more easily. They may come to you in dreams or intuitive nudges, where you just know that what you are experiencing right now is something from a past life (such as a fear or being about to repeat a pattern). You will be able to see your past lives as flashes of insight that come into your mind giving you vital pieces of information that you need for your current soul journey.

Let's end this chapter with looking at the akashic records, the storehouse of your soul.

The Akashic Records

The akashic records hold your entire soul's history – past, present and future. Every thought, emotion, observation, memory, idea, belief, decision, action, judgement, choice and experience that your soul has gone or will go through is held here alongside all of your soul contracts and past lives.

The word 'akasha' is a Sanskrit word that means ether, the primordial energy that is everything yet nothing and creates and connects everything. The akashic records exist in the higher realms of consciousness and are guarded by powerful beings of light. You may think of them like a metaphysical library that holds a vibrational archive of your entire soul's journey since the dawn of time.

Accessing the akashic records can give you deep insights and answers, and help you to make decisions, understand soul lessons and contracts, explore your past lives and learn more about yourself and your cosmic purpose.

To access the akashic records, it helps initially to go in with a particular question or intention as it narrows down your search and will help you to find what you are looking for more easily. You could ask about a particular situation you are going through or struggling with, insight into your purpose or whether something you are experiencing is related to a past life. Try working with just one question at a time to begin with as too many will confuse things and give your ego mind more reason to doubt.

Create your safe space and take a few moments with your eyes closed to ground and centre yourself (see page 34). Once you feel relaxed and ready, begin to meditate on the question that you are seeking answers to or guidance on. Ask for permission to enter the akashic records – this is a divine sacred space and needs to be treated with respect. Many times people will meet a guide or light being upon entering the records. If this happens to you, introduce yourself and ask your question again.

In the beginning it may help to visualise walking down a hall and accessing a big library with lots of ancient books. Perhaps allow yourself to be guided to a particular book, take it down, open it and see what it says.

Once you have finished your time in the akashic records, give thanks for the knowledge and wisdom you received (this may come at a later time) and close and seal the records once more. Once you come out of your meditation, immediately note down anything that you experienced.

The first few times that you do this you may not experience anything and that's ok – this all takes practice and patience and is part of your journey. Trust that you got what you needed, and it will make itself known to you when the time is right. Try to go in without any expectations or preconceived ideas (from your ego mind) and just practise deep listening and feeling, being open to receive whatever wants to come to you.

*

Now that you have a deeper understanding of what you came here to do in this lifetime, it's time to put that into practice by living a life that's true to you. Let's look at how you can do that now.

WHISPERS FROM YOUR SOUL

- ❍ Do you feel that you have lived lives before? What are your beliefs around past lives?
- ❍ What soul contracts do you intuitively feel you are working through in this lifetime?
- ❍ What questions do you want to take into your akashic records right now to have answered?

‘You need to be brave enough to live life on your terms and show others what’s possible when you live from your truth.’

Chapter 22

DARE TO LIVE A LIFE THAT'S TRUE TO YOU

So many people are living a life that is expected of them or following the pathway laid out for them by others. But you are not here to live the life that your parents or partner or society wants for you. You are here to live the life that your soul wants, and this is a huge part of your cosmic purpose.

The world around us is constantly telling us what we should be doing with our time or what we should be striving for or fighting for or caring about. We are fed misinformation about the kind of life we should want for ourselves and, if you don't have a clear plan for your life, others will make that plan for you. And then you end up living their version of your life and, in doing so, abandon your soul.

I know that initially this can feel like an extremely overwhelming thought, especially if you're a people-pleaser or have spent your whole life following the rules and doing what others have expected of you for so long. You may fear being abandoned or rejected and, worst of all, have no idea what a life that is true to you would even look like. But one of the biggest, bravest, boldest and most purposeful and inspiring things you can do is to dare to live a life that is true to you.

Getting to Know Yourself

Begin this journey gently. If you don't know what a life true to you would look like, begin with getting to know yourself. People often tell me that they don't know what they want or they don't know what their purpose is, and how can we ever if we don't even know ourselves? How can you possibly know what you want if you don't know who you are? Who you are is in there, it's just buried beneath a lifetime of trying to fit in, following others, living up to expectations or living a life on someone else's terms.

So, start small by asking yourself conscious questions:

- Do I agree with what is being said right now?
- Do I love the work that I do?
- If I was being true to me right now, would I say yes or no to this?
- Am I just agreeing with what is being said as I don't have an opinion of my own about this or want to avoid confrontation?
- What is my opinion about this?
- Am I doing this to impress someone?
- Do I really enjoy what I'm doing right now?
- What would I do right now if I were being true to myself?
- Am I being influenced by someone else and their opinions right now?
- Am I only doing this as I feel like I should?
- What would make me happy today?
- What do I need right now?

Living a life that's true to you means facing truths about yourself. Think about where you give away your power and outsource your opinions, views, worth, approval and validation. Consider how you allow others, social media, what society says or external motivation to lead your life and where you simply conform to what others expect of you. But is any of this what your soul wants?

What makes your soul come to life? Begin listening more to the voice of your soul and what makes you happy, brings you joy and feels true for you, and what it is that you actually believe and want. The more you get to know yourself, the easier this will become. Try new things, try on new beliefs and opinions, try doing things differently and see how it all fits. You don't initially need to share any of this with the outside world – begin by establishing your inner truth and being comfortable with that before you start to set those boundaries and show up differently on the outside. Because, when you do, you're going to need to risk being misunderstood and being seen as different to those around you and, honestly, that's truly what the world needs right now. The world doesn't need more people conforming and following the crowd. It needs more trailblazers – those who are unafraid to be who they are and who no longer buy into the outdated narratives that tell us how we should look or behave and what we should want for our lives.

Your soul can't help you to create the life that you are here for if you are living the life of someone else and what's expected of you. If you truly want to live a life of cosmic purpose, it's time to free yourself and throw off the shackles of the past, of expectations and 'should's, and instead dare to be different. You need to be brave enough to live life on your terms and show others what's possible when you live from your truth and your heart. Trust in what opportunities open up when you take the road less travelled and follow your unique soul's path.

Take me, for example. Imagine if I'd sat in front of the school career adviser and told them that I wanted to make a living out of teaching people to live by the magic of the moon and follow their soul's calling. I don't think that ever appeared on the list of possible career options, and I think that dream would have been quite quickly squashed and I'd have been told to be realistic. In fact, you have no idea the number of times over the last few decades I have been told to be realistic or have been ridiculed, doubted or underestimated. Yet, here I am, following the call of my soul, which has never led me astray.

It does take guts and a lot of trust and belief and daring to be different. Think of it like a silent disco – while everyone else has the same track playing in their ears, you're plugged into the song of your soul and beginning to move how your soul wants you to. The rest of the room is going to look at you and wonder why you're moving like that and not following the crowd. They may try to ridicule you or get you to conform to their dance, or even secretly envy you for doing your own thing. But they can't hear your soul's music and so it makes no sense to them, and it doesn't need to. They don't need to understand your dance and rhythm and flow, but you do. All you ever need to do in life is to listen to the whispers from your soul and dance to the music within you, living a life that's true to you.

As Dr Wayne Dyer once said, 'Don't die with your music still within you.' Don't get to the end of your life and realise that you lived it according to other people's expectations, denying your soul desires, being afraid to follow a dream or not doing what you know deep down you want to do. Please don't be afraid to dance to your own soul song. Please don't allow yourself to live any other life than the one your soul came here to live.

Life will always present us with people, situations, circumstances and lessons to show us where we are not free, where there is deeper work to be done and where we need to liberate ourselves from self-imposed or external expectations, judgements and bindings. Pay attention to where you feel the most restricted, stuck and held back as these are likely the life areas in which you are not being true to you.

What is really needed right now is more and more of us stepping into our full authentic selves and trusting and believing in ourselves, our souls and our ability to create the lives that we want – lives of meaning, purpose and fulfilment, whatever that means for you.

We have been led to believe that we can't make any difference in the world and, even worse, that life is meant to be a struggle, yet the reality is that we are powerful co-creators and the more of us who remember our divine power and follow our soul song to create lives that we want, the more we will inspire and guide others around us to do the same.

So, begin to live a life that is true to you. Be the one who goes first. Trust that anything you are being called to do, initiate, say, action and make happen is because it's part of your cosmic purpose and needed in the world. Listen to and trust your wants, needs and desires, and embrace your unique soul song. Your soul didn't come here to be anyone else; it came here to be you, bring what only you can offer and live a life that's true to you.

Stop following the crowd, saying the right thing, being the good girl or following convention, societal expectations or doing things the way they have always been done. Stop waiting for the world to change, or them to change, or them to approve, or them to say yes, or them to validate you before you can do what you want to do. Heal the wounds you have around being different, going first, believing in yourself and what you have to offer, and instead find the courage to be all of yourself and be true to you.

Be brave enough to live according to your own values, to speak your truth, to follow your own path and to be in alignment and integrity with your soul. Dare to live a life that's true to you.

You're now dancing to your soul song; I'm so happy for you. Let's look at more ways you can start to live your cosmic purpose now.

WHISPERS FROM YOUR SOUL

- ❍ Where are you not living a life that's true to you and why?
- ❍ Where is your soul song calling you? What would you do right now if you were being true to you and your soul?
- ❍ What would living a life that's true to you look and feel like?

‘Stop waiting for an imagined future when you’ll begin to live your cosmic purpose and start living it now.’

Chapter 23

START LIVING YOUR COSMIC PURPOSE NOW

One of the greatest ways that you can move towards more of your cosmic purpose is to simply start now. Stop waiting for the moment when you think you'll know more, or when it's all 'perfect', or when you do another course and get yet another qualification, or when you find the answers or get the solution or have it all figured out or something out there changes.

You can start living your cosmic purpose right now, in this very moment. You can decide that this moment is part of your cosmic purpose, and that your soul brought you to this exact moment, which it did, for a reason.

Your soul only exists in the present moment. In fact, your entire life only exists in the present moment. This moment, right now, as you are reading these words, is the only moment you ever really have. The past is gone. The future is imagined. So, stop waiting for an imagined future when you'll begin to live your cosmic purpose and start living it now.

This may begin by just believing that you have a purpose and something to offer to the world, just by being you, which you do. There is no one else in the world who has lived the life that you have lived, experienced what you have experienced or been through what you have been through. You have a unique perspective on the world and something to share and offer. So how can you begin to make a difference in your own family, community or workplace right now? This is part of your cosmic purpose. Yes, it's to awaken to your soul self and so much more, which we've been exploring in these pages, but it's also to show up as all of you and begin to make a difference in the lives and world around you – right now.

Starting Now

Even if it's not quite where you want to be, begin to see the job and relationships and situations you're currently in as part of your cosmic purpose. Look at what they are teaching you and how they are asking you to grow and leading you towards more of your purpose. Because everything in your life is part of your cosmic purpose. Your purpose is not some elusive thing out there that you need to chase and never quite catch. It's you, in this moment and this experience, and how you are navigating it (from your ego or soul) and how it's all shaping you and taking you closer to your soul. Your entire life is your cosmic purpose and, once you start to see it in this way, your life will change.

Very often, we don't begin something as the results or effects seem like a distant dream or too far away. But if you never start, you'll never get there. If you do nothing now that takes you towards where you want to go or who you want to grow into, then it will never happen. You have to start somewhere and there is no better time than now.

You have the power to change your life in this very moment. Stop waiting for life to happen and make it happen. Stop waiting for change and make a change. Stop waiting to be someone and become someone. As soon as you make one move, the universe can come and guide you the rest of the way and your soul can begin to weave in the experiences that you need to take you further towards where you want to go.

When you're waiting for this imaginary time when you'll find your purpose, or when the time will be right, or when it will all be perfect, you are standing still and letting life pass you by. Start now, today, with just one step in the direction of your dreams or towards more of your soul self and who you want to be. That may look like setting a boundary or making a phone call or showing up for yourself or choosing you.

Get honest about where you have been kidding yourself and promising that you'll start next week or next month or that things will get better or change soon, only keeping yourself stuck in situations and behaviours that, deep down, you know need to change.

If you do nothing about those things you aren't happy with in your life or where you are unfulfilled, don't feel like things are working or are stuck, then nothing at all will change and you'll get to the end of another year of your life where you've just let life happen to you.

So, start now. Look at what you want for yourself and your life, who you want to be and what you want your life to look like. Declare what you want. Don't just wish it, envision it or hope for it, but take back your power and declare it – loud and proud. Trust that you have within you what it takes to get there. Get honest about how that will require you to change or what you need to put your time, energy and focus into to make that happen.

You may not know how, and that's ok; you don't have to. Very often on the spiritual journey, we don't have all the 'how's, and we set out with a pocketful of trust and dreams. But the journey of starting now and moving towards what we want is what makes us into the version of us who can hold it when it arrives.

You don't need to do it all now, or even this week or this month. But you do need to do small things daily and make small changes and different choices that will take you towards where you want to go. And you need to start to do them now.

There may be the little voice that tells you that there are so many other people already doing what you want to do or that you don't know enough or do enough to make a difference in the world or it's not the right time or you'll wait until this, that or then – and this is showing you what will always hold you back if you allow it to. Because, honestly, there may be hundreds of other people doing what you want to do, but none of them will do it like you. We need you.

One final thing I'd like to mention here at the end of this chapter is that, very often, we don't start a meditation practice or daily rituals or connecting with our guides or any number of spiritual practices as we feel like we need to get it 'right' and perfect, and if it's not perfect, you can't do the rituals. You look to me or someone else to tell you exactly how your rituals should be as you feel like you have to get it 'right'.

This is yet another form of self-sabotage and something that will stop you from getting closer to your soul. Start now, simply, but start. You do know what to do; trust that you do. Begin with a five-minute timed meditation and a prayer to your soul to guide you. Begin with lighting a candle at the beginning of the day. Begin by asking your guides to help you with something. Start now and the journey will unfold before you.

You've started. It could be a small start, but it's a start and I'm so proud of you. Let's now look at how you can live as your soul self.

WHISPERS FROM YOUR SOUL

- What have you been putting off starting as you're waiting for something to happen or until it's perfect or until you have approval or permission from something outside of you? Where are you still holding back parts of you, waiting until you can be somebody?
- How is your current life situation part of your cosmic purpose? What is it teaching and showing you?
- Where do you put off doing rituals or practices that will take you closer to your soul as you feel you don't know how or they have to be perfect?

‘It’s time to acknowledge and express your gifts and really let yourself be seen and shine.’

Chapter 24

LIVING AS YOUR SOUL SELF

It's time to remember who you were before the world told you who to be. As each one of us awakens to the essence of our souls and our own value, brilliance and what we have to offer – and follows our intuition and the call of our soul – that's how we begin to live our cosmic purpose.

I urge you to start to know yourself as the beautiful, powerful, magical, magnetic, perfectly imperfect human and soul that you are. You have something to offer, you have something to give, you have something to share, you have something to say, you have a cosmic purpose – and we all need it.

It's time to fully shine your light; no more dimming, censoring, hiding or doubting. It's time to own all of you and what your soul came here to express and bring to life through you.

Many of you reading this may have felt like you never quite fitted in – you were always a bit too much or never quite enough, or you were an outcast or on the fringes of society and had to alter or dim or shrink certain parts of yourself to fit into the mainstream, but now it's your time.

Being All of You

We are going through one of the biggest consciousness shifts in humanity that we have been through and, in order to create a new world, we need more and more of us beginning to live as the souls that we are and allowing our souls to experience life through this human experience.

Notice if any fears are coming up for you about what you have to offer the world and your talents, gifts, psychic abilities, intuition or simply allowing yourself to be free to be all of you. If you want to play your part in where the world goes next, it's so important to recognise and heal these things.

One of the greatest ways to begin to live as your soul self and what your soul came here for is to go within and, from a deep soul level (not the opinion of your ego), look at who you want to be and what you want from your life. What are your deep soul longings and desires and the soul nudges that simply won't go away? Sit in the vibration of your soul and let your soul show you.

All the world ever truly needs and the only way to live your cosmic purpose is for you to be YOU – not some watered down or censored version of you or who you think they or I want you to be. But to be you – the you that you came here to be.

Feel the frequency of your soul within you, feel your own unique essence. Allow that to begin to expand and shine and radiate from you, and then begin to live as your soul. Live as though what you want is already here. Live as the you your soul wishes you to be.

All the world needs now is you being all of you and bringing all of you to everything you do; you listening to and trusting your wants, needs and desires, and embracing your unique soul energy.

Your soul didn't come here to be anyone else; it came here to be you and bring what only you can offer.

It's time to fully claim all of yourself and to believe in yourself and what you have to offer like never before. You need to play your part. Look at anyone who has ever touched or affected your life in any way and imagine if they hadn't followed the intuitive niggle or the call of their soul. Your life would not have been affected in the same way.

If you feel that my books or content have changed or shaped your life in any way, imagine if I had let the little voice of doubt (which, believe me, is very loud at times!) stop me from sharing what I do or being who I am. Your life would not have been affected in the same way.

In just the same way, if you ignore the nudges, niggles, calls or just not allow yourself to be all of you, there will be many, many people out there whose lives will not be affected in the ways they could be by YOU.

This is not a time to shrink, dim or play small. It's a time to acknowledge and express your gifts and really let yourself be seen and shine. We need your unique light and what you can offer in the world, and you dimming and hiding helps no one.

You have something to offer to the world right now just by being you. So, begin to do that. Show up in the way that only you can and make a difference in the way that only you can. Let your soul be expressed through you and allow your soul gifts to be shared with the world.

The more you begin to do this, the more your cosmic purpose can make its way to you – you'll see solutions where there were problems and answers where there were questions, and synchronicities and signs happen. Life just flows as you remember who you truly are – you are a soul having a human experience. You are pure divine consciousness. You are 1 in 8 billion. You are the entire universe in a human body.

Please, my love, begin to remember how truly magical, unique and perfect you are. The world needs your unique, individual soul's light. Let all of you shine.

WHISPERS FROM YOUR SOUL

- ❍ What do you have to offer to the world just by being you?
- ❍ If you truly believed that you were a soul having a human experience, how would that change how you live and show up in the world?
- ❍ Who would you allow yourself to be if you were going to be all of you?

PART 3
ASTROLOGY FOR YOUR COSMIC PURPOSE

We now move into Part 3, where you get to explore astrology and your own birth chart to help you to find a deeper understanding of your cosmic purpose.

‘Exploring your birth chart gives you a better understanding of you and your soul’s journey in this lifetime.’

Chapter 25

EXPLORE YOUR BIRTH CHART TO UNCOVER WHAT MAKES YOU YOU

Your birth chart is a wonderful place to explore if you want to uncover more of your cosmic purpose. We say that things are written in the stars and, when it comes to your birth chart, they are. Your birth chart is a snapshot of the skies and where all the planets were at the time you were born. (You can create a free birth chart on my website: www.kirstygallagher.com.)

If you ever find yourself wondering what you are here for or what your purpose is, or needing to understand more about what is happening during a certain period of your life, you will find many of these answers and so much more in your birth chart.

Your soul chooses the exact moment to come to earth based on your chart, so you can think of your birth chart like a blueprint or map of your journey and purpose in this lifetime (and lifetimes before) that your soul has laid out for you.

The placement of each planet in each sign in each house and each aspect in astrology has a unique influence and purpose in our lives. They each hold different positive and challenging energies, traits, lessons and opportunities for growth, and this is why your soul chose this particular birth chart for you. Learning more about your chart can give you insights into your truest, most authentic self, alongside obstacles you may face and things you need to learn and overcome, helping you to understand you and your life path in a more profound way.

Your chart will not only speak to you of what you came here to do and who you came here to be, but it can also give you guidance on how your soul came here to grow and evolve and, even more importantly, contribute to the world in the unique way that only you can.

I know that, for me, learning about my own birth chart helped me to know and understand myself so much more and gave me permission to be all of me. It answered so many questions about why I am the way I am and helped me to overcome challenges and accept and embrace all of me, realising the best version of me that I can be.

Of course, that is an ongoing process, but that's the beauty of astrology; the planets are always in motion and these transits are constantly working with our birth chart, helping us to face and shed layers of ourselves, grow into more of our soul self and complete more of our soul contracts.

There will be more on transits in Chapter 27. For now, let's explore what you can look for in your birth chart to give you a better understanding of you and your soul's journey in this lifetime.

The Big Three

We'll begin with your 'big three' as these are the building blocks of what make you YOU. The big three refers to your sun sign, moon sign and rising sign (or ascendant). These are the blueprint to your personality traits, your vibes, your behaviours, your likes and dislikes, your emotional world and how you move through the world.

Your big three work together to make you all of who you are and, by embracing all of these sides of you, you can understand, love, honour and accept yourself and show up in the world as more of who your soul wants you to be.

For example, you may have an Aquarius sun, Taurus moon and Gemini rising. Your Aquarius sun makes you freedom-seeking and rebellious while your Taurus moon brings a need for stability, routine and ritual, which can feel conflicting and a struggle if you don't embrace and accept all these parts of you. Embracing your moon's need for stability will mean that your Aquarius sun can feel free to adventure, with a plan. Or that you'll be a much more effective rebel when you're well rested and nourished. In among all of this, your Gemini rising will come across as curious and restless and make you a wonderful communicator.

A Leo sun, Scorpio moon and Libra rising would be someone who has a big heart and loves to be the centre of attention and shine brightly, while their Scorpio moon needs plenty of alone time and privacy and can feel easily overwhelmed by too much time in the spotlight. Their Libra rising means the world sees someone who's balanced, harmonious and calm.

Your sun sign: How you're here to shine and light up the world

Most of us know our sun sign (sometimes referred to as star or zodiac sign). This is where the sun was when you were born. Made popular in pop astrology, where a few lines in a newspaper presume to be able to tell you about how your day will go, your sun sign holds so much power in helping you begin to understand how you are here to shine in the world.

Your sun sign is your sense of self, core personality, identity and how you move through the world. It represents your inner essence and how you can find most fulfilment, joy and authentic self-expression, which, in turn, will guide you towards more of your cosmic purpose. Just like our earthly sun is the giver of life and light on our planet, your sun sign shows where you give light and life to the people and world around you.

Your sun sign is how you came here to shine in this lifetime, and learning more about it will help you to understand yourself and who you are growing into on a deeper level. Embracing the qualities of your sun sign will help you to begin to show up, be seen and shine as your most authentic self and radiate more of yourself into the world, allowing the light of your soul to begin to shine through.

As well as embodying and embracing the positive traits and characteristics of your sun sign, part of your journey is to overcome and learn from the more challenging ones, leading you on a voyage of self-exploration, self-study and self-knowing.

Your sun sign, for example, may help you to understand and work on your perfectionist tendencies that may keep you from putting yourself or your work out there in the world until it's 'perfect' (which it never will be!). Alternatively, your sun sign may highlight your stubborn streak that could cause you to sabotage or miss certain opportunities or your tendency to overthink things to the point of exhaustion or start a hundred things and never complete one. It also shows you ways that you may dim your shine.

The list below will give you a simple overview of suggested

ways in which you're here to shine and what you need to overcome to ensure that you're not dimming your soul's light.

Aries

How you're here to shine: a natural born leader, you are here to take charge, take risks and make things happen. You are the ultimate hype person with the gift of being able to make anyone feel like anything is possible. You bring enthusiasm, high energy and passion to everything that you do.

What you need to overcome: childish temper tantrums and being moody and irrational, especially when things don't go your way. You may also need to tame your impulsive tendencies, learn patience and be a little less confrontational and cut-throat. You have a habit of starting 100 things and never finishing one, so you need to learn to see things through.

Taurus

How you're here to shine: warm, dependable and genuine, you have the ability to make everyone around you feel welcome, safe and taken care of. You have a deep connection to the senses and are skilled at creating cosy, luxurious, comfortable spaces and bringing a soothing aura to any environment. You teach everyone around you to slow down and connect to the pleasure of the present moment.

What you need to overcome: your stubbornness – this can often be your downfall. You have a huge resistance to any kind of change, staying in situations you've long outgrown just because they feel familiar and comfortable. This also means that, at times, you can miss seeing the bigger picture and let things pass you by as you're slow to act. There can be a tendency for overindulgence, so you need to learn moderation.

Gemini

How you're here to shine: known for your quick wit and intellect, you have a brilliant mind that works like no other with thoughts that need to be shared. You have an insatiable curiosity for life and are fascinated by everyone and everything around you, wanting to explore and experience it all. An excellent communicator, you easily connect with others through your words.

What you need to overcome: getting so easily bored that you simply flit from one thing to the next in life (jobs, relationships, homes, and so on) without ever being consistent and dedicated to one thing. You can often act impulsively without thinking about the consequences and need to learn to manage your mood swings, which can be quite extreme.

Cancer

How you're here to shine: the caretaker of the zodiac, you are known for your empathy, compassion and ability to nurture, comfort and support others in just the way that they need it. You are deeply intuitive and highly sensitive to emotions and energies, easily able to read rooms and people.

What you need to overcome: being cold and distant and hiding in your shell, especially when you feel vulnerable. You tend to hold on to the past and grudges, and can be clingy, finding it hard to move on. You can also at times be overbearing and put the needs of others above your own.

Leo

How you're here to shine: ruled by the sun and ruler of the heart, you are here to spread warmth and love and let your Leo light shine on all those you meet. You have an infectious energy, a big heart, a wonderful way with words and are a natural leader, celebrating others and helping them to get to where they want to go. You want to be recognised for being your authentic self and will in turn recognise the same in others.

What you need to overcome: masking your inner insecurities. A lot of your outer confidence is actually a mask and you are easily hurt. You need to learn to validate yourself rather than looking for it from others. You aren't good at showing vulnerability or asking for help and cannot stand being told what to do. You can be impatient, wanting it all now, and need to learn to trust the journey.

Virgo

How you're here to shine: your organisational skills are second to none and there is no problem too big for you to able to solve. You pay attention to the smallest detail and can bring any dream down into reality, making just about anything happen when you put your heart and soul into it.

What you need to overcome: your inner critic. This could hold you back from, well, most things in life if you let it, as will your need for things to be perfect. You also tend to worry about everything and make mountains out of molehills, and can be judgemental and overly critical, with yourself and others.

Libra

How you're here to shine: you bring balance, harmony and peace to the world around you. A natural diplomat, you have a confident, calm way that creates an atmosphere of comfort and ease which everyone gets to bask in. You have a knack of making people feel special and you're brilliant at seeing all sides of any situation and bringing people together.

What you need to overcome: your people-pleasing and co-dependency tendencies. Learning how to make a decision and not sit on the fence is one of your greatest life lessons. You avoid conflict at any cost, even if that means foregoing your own needs and desires.

Scorpio

How you're here to shine: your intuitive and psychic skills are unmatched, and you are here to make the invisible visible and bring the truth to light. You are not afraid of the emotional depths and live life with an intense desire for deeper understanding and uncovering life's mysteries.

What you need to overcome: being secretive and overly suspicious. You tend to have a deep mistrust for everything and everyone, and you also have a possessive, controlling streak. This can become manipulative if you feel like you're losing power.

Sagittarius

How you're here to shine: the adventurer, traveller and wanderer of the zodiac, you are here to explore all that life has to offer and have a deep desire for gathering wisdom and knowledge. You exude optimism and playfulness and bring out the best in everyone.

What you need to overcome: thinking that you know best, about everything. This can come across as egotistical and arrogant. You're known for your truth-telling, but this can verge on being blunt and tactless at times. You can also be a real commitment-phobe and unreliable at times.

Capricorn

How you're here to shine: your ambition knows no bounds and you make a huge success of anything that you put your heart and mind to, breaking down the journey into small, manageable steps. You know your true potential and will do all that you can to live up to it and give your all to everything you do.

What you need to overcome: putting your big expectations on to others, which often leaves you feeling disappointed. Not everyone is as ambitious and motivated as you, so be mindful of that. In a similar way, part of your learning is to not put too many unrealistic expectations on yourself, leaving you striving but never arriving.

Aquarius

How you're here to shine: the revolutionary freedom-seekers of the zodiac, you are here to shake things up, progress things along and make the world a better place. You don't like to follow the rules; instead, you make up new ones as you go along, inspiring others to do the same. You're an inventor and innovator, solving problems and doing things in ways they haven't been done before.

What you need to overcome: rebelling just for rebellion's sake and being 'all or nothing' in everything you do. You can also be cold and distant, even ruthless, at times, struggling to express your emotions, and you have a real sarcastic side to your humour.

You can get bored easily, sometimes creating drama just to shake things up.

Pisces

How you're here to shine: a natural born dreamer with a vivid imagination, you have an intuitive understanding of life and all those around you. You are a true empath and an old soul, able to feel what others are feeling and give the best care, support and advice to all who need it. You're an artist, a creative, weaving the mystical and spiritual into all that you do.

What you need to overcome: escapism, avoidance and even overindulgence to escape the 'real world'. You can get utterly consumed by your emotions if you allow yourself to, and the emotions of others, which you readily soak up. One of your big life lessons is implementing boundaries and protecting your energy, and not allowing yourself to be taken advantage of.

Your moon sign: How you need to nourish your soul

Whereas your sun sign shows you how to shine your light out into the world, your moon sign shines that light within you, showing you who you truly are on the inside and all that goes on beneath the surface. It's your inner world, your subconscious and who you are when no one else is watching.

Your moon sign teaches you about what nourishes your soul and how you need to care for yourself to feel safe and at home in the world and more whole, content and purposeful in yourself and your life. When you nurture and look after your moon and her needs and desires, your sun can shine so much more brightly.

Your moon teaches you how to access your intuition and

instincts, and the soul dreams and desires within you. It teaches you about your 'why' and what deeply motivates you and makes you happy. It's your emotional world and your emotional responses to the world around you, and gives insight into what you need from relationships in your life and how you navigate love and romance.

Your moon also teaches you about your deep vulnerabilities and defence mechanisms and the parts of you that you hide which prevent you from expressing yourself fully. It shows you how to tend to your soul to prevent emotional outbursts, burnout and exhaustion. It may help to think of your moon like your inner child – the part of you that can feel neglected and needs taking care of.

Understanding your inner emotional world and what makes you tick is the key to knowing and trusting all of yourself and beginning to live more of your soul purpose. Learning about your moon sign helps you to understand who you truly are, what you need, how you feel and why you feel the way that you feel.

The list below will give you a simple overview of suggested ways to nourish your soul and how you can tend to your emotions to express yourself fully.

Aries

Nourish your soul by: trying something new, going on an adventure or taking action and going after something that you want. This will feed your innate need for independence, personal freedom and to do things your own way.

Tend to your emotions by: learning to respond not react and finding an outlet (like physical exercise) to release any pent-up frustrations so they don't build up and overwhelm you. This will help you to counter your hot-headedness, where otherwise you would be quick to react, acting on your emotional impulses and wanting what you want in the moment that you want it.

Taurus

Nourish your soul by: taking care of yourself and having routines and rituals in your life that help you to feel grounded and connected. You feel most at home when things are calm and stable and you can take things at your own pace, follow your own natural rhythm and do things your own way in your own time.

Tend to your emotions by: fully opening up and being vulnerable. You have deep-rooted insecurities and, when you get tired, drained or overwhelmed, you can tend to completely emotionally shut down and shut out the world and/or overindulge.

Gemini

Nourish your soul by: discovering and learning new things, finding answers and figuring things out. You crave information, learning and to know and experience as much as you possibly can. You also have a childlike nature and love to play and have fun.

Tend to your emotions by: feeling your feelings and getting acquainted with your emotional needs. You're not very good at feeling your emotions (you prefer to talk about them), so you sometimes find it hard to understand your own needs and this can easily lead to burnout when you don't take proper care of yourself.

Cancer

Nourish your soul by: listening to and following your own inner rhythm and honouring what you feel like doing daily (or even hourly!), depending on your moods. You have a deep need for a place to call home and to connect with, nurture and care for those you love, and you will thrive when you are able to trust and follow your intuition.

Tend to your emotions by: learning to recognise the difference between your emotions and the emotions of others. When you end up emotionally drained, you tend to withdraw into your shell and not let anyone or anything in, so be sure to take care of yourself as well as you take care of everyone else.

Leo

Nourish your soul by: expressing yourself, your creativity and your emotions in a healthy way that feels meaningful to you. You need to be able to put your heart into all that you do and enjoy play and adventures. You thrive off helping others to be their best self.

Tend to your emotions by: learning to give yourself the praise, appreciation and validation that you look for from outside of you. On the outside, you may appear confident, arrogant even, but inside you're often riddled with self-doubt and can be easily hurt.

Virgo

Nourish your soul by: having a daily routine, structure and organisation in your life. With your moon in Virgo, you desire feeling needed and useful in the world, and you love nothing more than to be of service and to help and improve the lives of all those around you.

Tend to your emotions by: recognising that you're always doing your best. You can be your own worst critic and constantly fear not being enough. You can also bring too much reason and logic to your emotions, so it's important to lean into and trust your emotions and intuition a little more.

Libra

Nourish your soul by: staying balanced in your body, mind and heart. You need equilibrium in your life, and the first sign of anything becoming unbalanced can easily make you spiral and send you off track. Make sure that you are regularly nurturing, caring for yourself and taking care of your needs with self-care practices.

Tend to your emotions by: learning about healthy conflict, boundaries and facing issues head on. You're good at dealing with other people's big emotions, just not your own, fearing being disliked or judged for being open about your emotions. With your desire to be liked and please others, you can struggle with indecision and find it hard to face issues, but doing so creates more conflict and often resentment.

Scorpio

Nourish your soul by: setting yourself ambitious goals and working towards them, particularly if you get to make a significant impact on others along the way. You like to confront things head on, get to the truth and work through challenges, seeing them as an opportunity for growth and discovery.

Tend to your emotions by: taking plenty of alone time. You are so sensitive to energy and emotions that you need to give yourself time to process, integrate and recover. Make sure that you have healthy outlets for your big emotions, such as meditation, journaling, somatic practices or therapy.

Sagittarius

Nourish your soul by: trusting and following your instincts and allowing them to guide you forwards in life. You need to have the freedom to live life on your own terms and have a deep desire for freedom, adventure, to embrace the unknown and be able to follow where your heart wants you to go.

Tend to your emotions by: not trying to 'love and light' your way out of anything uncomfortable and instead taking time to understand your emotions and why you feel the way you do, so that you can use this for self-development and growth.

Capricorn

Nourish your soul by: implementing routines and discipline, which help you to keep it all together and thrive. It helps for you to always have a long-term goal or ambition that you are working on, giving you something to focus on and strive towards. You also gain a lot of purpose from being the leader or provider.

Tend to your emotions by: learning to express and process or even share your emotions rather than compartmentalising or avoiding them. Take care not to overlook how you're feeling in favour of your goals and responsibilities.

Aquarius

Nourish your soul by: making a difference in the world and having a deep desire to contribute to change and make the world a better place. You need to be free to be truly yourself, embracing your uniqueness, making your own rules and going your own way.

Tend to your emotions by: learning to take care of your stress levels so that things don't get too overwhelming. Emotionally quite detached, you're not big on overly emotional situations, prefer logic over intuition and like to think your emotions rather than feel them, so much so that you can often get lost in your thoughts and spend way too much time overthinking things.

Pisces

Nourish your soul by: having a daily connection to the divine, whether that's through meditation, time in nature, feeling a sense of oneness or studying the meaning of life in some way. You also gain a lot of meaning from helping and offering support to those around you (as long as you are taking steps to protect yourself and your energy).

Tend to your emotions by: learning to realise what are others' emotions and what are yours. You tend to be like a sponge, soaking up the energy and emotions from everyone around you, and this can leave you feeling overwhelmed, so it's essential that you take regular time alone and time out to prevent becoming world-weary and losing yourself.

Your rising sign or ascendant: The window to your soul

This is the sign that was rising on the eastern horizon when you were born. It changes every two hours, which is why you need to know the time of your birth to get this accurate.

Your rising sign teaches you about the way you see and interact with the world around you and the energy with which you move through the world. It is the version of you who you project to the outside world and who other people meet. You may say it's the window to your soul. It's the part of you that you let others see easily and the vibe that others will immediately pick up about you.

This explains how others can often see you differently to how you see yourself and also how when you meet someone you can think they are a certain way, but when you really get to know them, you realise they are someone quite different to your first impression.

Deeper than that, your rising sign shows you more about how you're here to evolve in this lifetime and determines your soul purpose and how your soul will express and manifest into the world through you. It's how you rise into your purpose and embrace your soul lessons, and gives deep insight into who you are at a soul level.

The list below will give you a simple insight into how you can rise into more of your soul purpose and how you're seen in the world.

Aries

You're here to inspire and lead by being the one who goes first and trailblazing new pathways forwards. You are seen as assertive, independent and, sometimes, a bit pushy and impatient. Part of your purpose is to really know and trust yourself and take charge of your own destiny, taking the first bold, brave step and trusting that the next one will appear.

Taurus

You're here to ground the spiritual world into reality and blend the metaphysical with the physical. You are seen as patient, calm and easy-going, and sometimes extremely stubborn. Part of your purpose is to let go of attachment to the material world and enjoy the simple pleasures in life and to trust your intuition to guide you to a higher, more meaningful purpose.

Gemini

You're here to communicate, explore ideas, learn, share knowledge and wisdom and connect others. You are seen as someone with a sharp mind who is curious, energetic and engaging, and sometimes a bit restless and distracted. Part of your purpose is to balance the wisdom of your head and your heart and to learn open, direct communication from a place of truth.

Cancer

You're here to feel and nurture, care for and love everyone around you, creating a sense of true belonging. You are seen as caring, compassionate and motherly, and sometimes a bit moody and smothering. Part of your purpose is to take care of others without forgetting about yourself and to learn emotional intelligence, gaining the wisdom from your emotions without them consuming you.

Leo

You're here to shine brightly and express your unique soul self and teach others how to do the same. You light up a room when you enter it. You're seen as confident, charismatic and warm, and sometimes a bit over the top and dramatic. Part of your purpose is overcoming your ego and learning to love and appreciate yourself without needing the approval of the outside world and to follow your heart.

Virgo

You're here to be of service and to be a true expression of the divine through your work, helping to heal both yourself and others.

You're seen as organised, intelligent and practical, and sometimes critical and controlling. Part of your purpose is in accepting human flaws and letting go of criticism and perfectionism, realising it's all perfect in the eyes of your soul.

Libra

You're here to bring balance and harmony to the world, especially through relationships. You're seen as charming, gentle and a peacemaker, and sometimes avoidant or a people-pleaser. Part of your purpose is learning to be in the right relationship with yourself first and to find the peace and harmony you are looking for within you.

Scorpio

You're here to explore the depths of life, emotion and transformation, and to alchemise darkness into light and help others do the same. You're seen as intense, magnetic and mysterious, and sometimes aloof and closed off. Part of your purpose is in self-mastery and learning how to wield your incredible power for good and to keep rising from the ashes of your transformations.

Sagittarius

You're here to explore new beliefs and ways of life, and to help humanity ascend through sharing your truth, wisdom and teachings. You're seen as optimistic, playful and fun-loving, and sometimes confrontational and stubborn in your beliefs. Part of your purpose is to help others find their beliefs and to seek wisdom and spiritual growth through your life experiences.

Capricorn

You're here to achieve your ambitions and to make the world a better place by doing so. You're seen as a hard worker, disciplined and determined, and sometimes a bit too serious and all work and no play. Part of your purpose is to live your spiritual calling through your work and create a legacy that inspires others to do the same, showing how to bring the sacred into business.

Aquarius

You're here to be of service to humanity, challenge what's seen as 'normal' and create progressive change in the world around you. You're seen as eccentric, unusual and unique, and sometimes detached and standoffish. Part of your purpose is to trust your intuition over your logical mind a little more, listening to your heart over your head.

Pisces

You're here to bring compassion, understanding and unconditional love to the world. You're seen as caring, wise and intuitive, and sometimes overly sensitive and living in a dream world. Part of your purpose is to dedicate yourself to others without losing yourself and to master your own emotions so that you can teach others about how to hold and understand theirs.

Now that you've come to understand more of what makes you YOU, let's explore what you can look for in your birth chart to give you a deeper understanding of your cosmic purpose as it's written in the stars.

‘The nodes of destiny or fate are there to help guide you along the path towards your cosmic purpose.’

Chapter 26

FIND YOUR COSMIC PURPOSE IN YOUR BIRTH CHART

Let's now look at other placements you can look for in your birth chart to help you to understand your cosmic purpose in a deeper way.

The Lunar Nodes

The lunar nodes are not physical bodies, but the points at which the pathway of the sun and moon interject. They come as a pair, with the north node always opposite the south node. Often called the nodes of destiny or nodes of fate, they tell you where you have been and where you are heading. They are the pathway towards more of your cosmic purpose and help you to unlock your destiny. They show you more about the experiences and lessons that your soul wants to have and the gifts that you are here to develop and share.

Your south node represents past lives and what you have already learned and mastered. It's the gifts that you've brought into this lifetime and what you're instinctively good at. But it's also your comfort zone and what you always slip back into that keeps you from truly growing into your cosmic purpose. It's what you need to learn from and move beyond in this lifetime.

Your north node is your north star, cosmic compass and what you're moving towards, which very often feels scary and unfamiliar as you haven't been there before. Your north node calls you towards all that your soul knows you can be and the future possibilities and pathways of your greatest purpose and evolution.

The journey from the comfort zone of your south node to the unknown of your north node is going to feel uncomfortable and as though it stretches and expands you, but this is the point. This journey and the lessons and challenges that you encounter on the way are how your soul grows and expands into the north node version of you.

Below is an idea of what you are here to grow towards and move beyond . . .

Aries north node/Libra south node

- **Grow towards:** finding your own way in life and forging your own path forward, becoming independent and being the leader.
- **Move beyond:** needing to always be part of the crowd, people-pleasing and always worrying about offending or upsetting others.

Taurus north node/Scorpio south node

- **Grow towards:** finding inner safety, stability and self-worth, loyalty to yourself, enjoying the simple pleasures in life and embracing presence.

- **Move beyond:** mistrusting the world and everyone in it (including yourself at times), fear of betrayal and being overly secretive.

Gemini north node/Sagittarius south node

- **Grow towards:** learning how to communicate and express yourself effectively, making connections and being curious about life and its meaning.
- **Move beyond:** being judgemental and intolerant of different beliefs and behaviours, fear of commitment and being a know-it-all.

Cancer north node/Capricorn south node

- **Grow towards:** embracing and trusting your emotions, intuition and feminine energies, being vulnerable and creating a safe space within you.
- **Move beyond:** feeling a duty towards everyone else and not taking care of yourself, being a workaholic and focusing too much on career goals over wellbeing.

Leo north node/Aquarius south node

- **Grow towards:** stepping into the spotlight and taking centre stage in your life, gaining self-confidence and courage, having fun and healing your inner child.
- **Move beyond:** putting aside your needs and dreams for the sake of others, giving more of yourself than you have to give, disassociating and closing yourself off.

Virgo north node/Pisces south node

- **Grow towards:** serving humanity in a meaningful way, embracing structure and discipline to reach your goals and make your dreams a reality.
- **Move beyond:** dreaming your dreams without putting them into action, getting too lost in the spiritual world to escape reality and self-doubt and self-defeating behaviours.

Libra north node/Aries south node

- **Grow towards:** creating balance, peace and harmony in your life, co-operation and collaboration with others, and growth through relationships.
- **Move beyond:** selfish tendencies where you put yourself first and want things your way, lack of compromise, being too self-reliant and impulsive tendencies.

Scorpio north node/Taurus south node

- **Grow towards:** letting go of anything that doesn't support your soul's growth, connection to the spiritual realms, confronting fears and embracing the mysteries of life.
- **Move beyond:** being overly attached to the material world and money, lack of self-worth, overindulgence and resistance to change.

Sagittarius north node/Gemini south node

- **Grow towards:** learning and seeking knowledge and wisdom, exploring the world and embracing adventure, and trusting in your higher self and intuition.
- **Move beyond:** getting stuck in limiting beliefs or negative thought patterns, getting overly caught up in the details and rushing through life.

Capricorn north node/Cancer south node

- **Grow towards:** taking charge of your life and going after your goals, being independent and self-sufficient, and pursuing a career that's meaningful and provides purpose.
- **Move beyond:** feeling responsible for everyone else and prioritising their needs over your own, needing to be needed and having no boundaries.

Aquarius north node/Leo south node

- **Grow towards:** making your own rules and being individual and authentic, making a difference to the world around you and inspiring others.
- **Move beyond:** being self-centred, needing admiration and validation from the outside world and allowing your pride to get in the way.

Pisces north node/Virgo south node

- **Grow towards:** trusting and living by your intuition and inner knowing, letting go of control and flowing with life, and exploring the spiritual realms.
- **Move beyond:** perfectionism and self-criticism, being stuck in routines and rigid rules about life and always needing a plan.

Eclipses: A Course Correction for Your Soul

This brings me to talk about eclipses, which can be thought of as a course correction for your soul. Eclipses happen when we get a new or full moon near one of the lunar nodes. Eclipses tend to happen twice a year and come in seasons, during which there will be two or three eclipses (one solar, one lunar and occasionally one more of either one). As this happens, all of our individual lunar nodes are activated and our soul gets to nudge us back on track.

Eclipses are times of huge evolution, change and transformation. They are soul portals where the universe can show you where you are out of alignment, integrity and congruence with your soul's path and destiny. They are often times of big change, crumbling and big endings and beginnings, with things eclipsing into and out of your life.

Lunar eclipses / eclipses on the south node bring endings and release, as the full moon shines a huge illuminating light on your life and shows you where you are gripping, clinging, holding on and staying too much in your comfort zone, not allowing yourself to grow and expand. They help to release what is not meant for you that is keeping you out of alignment with your soul journey.

Solar eclipses/eclipses on the north node are a powerful point of new beginnings, propelling you back on to your soul path. During a solar eclipse, you can sometimes be confronted with a sense of 'Who am I?' and a jarring realisation of where and how you have lost yourself.

The energy of eclipses can often be quite deep and intense, but they are powerful portals for huge transformation and opportunities for growth. How much eclipses affect you depends on how far you have strayed from your soul's path and how much your soul needs to course-correct you.

Please do remember that everything happening during eclipse portals is for your own highest good and your soul would not bring you anything you can't handle or that wasn't for your growth and to eventually take you to where you are meant to be.

I also want to point out here, and I need you to listen to me and really hear me, that nothing that is meant for you will be eclipsed out of your life. If it is meant to stay for the longer term, it will; it may just change form in some way.

But if it's not meant to be, if you're clinging on to something that isn't serving you or pushing doors that aren't yours or staying somewhere you're not meant to be, the eclipses will come in to help realign and reorient you back in alignment with your soul's path.

And this is where the surrender comes in: the more you can rest, receive and surrender to the energy of these eclipses, the more the universe can take care of you and carry you to where your soul needs you to be.

You can also choose to ignore the call of eclipses and your destiny; you have free will after all. But the more you ignore these little signposts from the universe, the more unfulfilling, frustrating and unhappy your life will likely become. My best advice is to open your heart, mind and arms wide and embrace eclipses with full trust.

Below are a few other placements that are worth looking into in your chart to give you more idea of your purpose and life path. Look at the sign and house of these to give you deeper insight.

Midheaven

Your midheaven (or MC) helps you to reach your full potential and follow your life's calling when it comes to your career and professional destiny. It gives clues to your natural talents, your public persona and how you can contribute to society. It's your highest calling and ambition and shows you what you can achieve. A beautiful way in which it is often described is the legacy that you're here to leave behind in this lifetime.

Pluto

Your Pluto placement gives insights into your soul's intention and how you're here to evolve, transform and grow in this lifetime. It shows where you find deeper meaning in your life and how you can step into your highest spiritual truth and power, finding your path in life.

It can teach you about past lives, core life themes and lessons for this lifetime that your soul has chosen to help you to evolve. Pluto also shows you where you resist change and is often the planet responsible for the death, rebirth and transformation process that brings down our egos and takes us closer to our souls.

Saturn

Your Saturn placement can give insight into the struggles and difficult life lessons that your soul has chosen for you to master and overcome as part of your soul's growth. These will be lessons that will come up over and over until you face and take responsibility for them and do the necessary work to transcend them.

Saturn is the teacher and taskmaster who helps you to 'grow up' from your ego into your soul and find the discipline to move towards your spiritual path. Once you learn to master Saturn in your chart and use the lessons and transits for inner transformation, you'll begin to fulfil so much more of your soul's destiny and mature into more of your soul self.

Now you've discovered what to look for in your birth chart, let's discuss some of the astrological transits that will help you to expand and grow into more of your cosmic purpose.

'Your soul, the planets and the stars all want to see you in your highest potential doing what you came here to do.'

Chapter 27

ASTROLOGY SOUL SCHOOL

In this final chapter, I want to share with you some of the more challenging astrological times that we all experience in life and how these are actually brilliant opportunities for soul growth.

As we saw in Chapter 25, your birth chart represents where all the planets were at the time you were born. But the planets are in constant movement, and the position they are in at any given time will likely make aspects (or connections) to the planets in your own chart. This is what's known as a transit, as current planets 'transit' planets in your birth chart.

The first thing that I need to explain here is that, contrary to popular belief, astrology and astrological transits do not cause or make us do anything. They simply reflect something that is already within you, pushing you to face something you've been avoiding, or bringing chaos into a life area that, deep down, you know hasn't been working for a long time.

Your soul, the planets and the stars all want what is best for you. They want to see you in your highest potential doing what you came here to do. Remember that, when you came to earth, your soul chose this birth chart with these transits for you, so everything in your chart and the skies is there to help you grow and become all that you can be.

When challenging transits come along and our life is seemingly thrown into turmoil, it can be difficult for human us to make sense of and understand what is happening, and this in turn makes things harder as we tend to resist and struggle and push and question. But if in these times you can instead lean into the part of you who knows, the soul part of you who chose this chart and these transits for your highest good, growth and potential, you'll navigate these times so much more easily.

Very often, there is a part of you who, deep down, was aware that things weren't right or in alignment or in flow, and that change was necessary and needed.

In a similar way to the Cosmic Weather Reports I have been sharing on my social channels for the last few years, knowing about these transits helps you to be prepared and navigate what's to come with more ease and grace, and less dread and uncertainty.

In the same way that you may take an umbrella out with you if you knew it was likely to rain or a warm coat if you knew it could get cold, knowing these transits are coming helps you to be as prepared as you can be. Of course, it may not rain, and your transits may not affect you in quite the way you expected them to, but at least you're ready.

Transits are happening all the time – and so if ever you're feeling a bit 'off', it may be worth a quick look at what's happening in your chart – but there are some that can have more impact than others and we'll look at these below. The ages I've included below are approximate – to find definite dates, you need to consult an astrologer and get your birth chart read (or be adept at reading your own chart).

Many of the big life-changing astrological transits happen

in our late thirties/early forties, which at least means we get to blame the skies for our midlife crisis! Seriously though, this is such a hugely transitional and transformational time of life where we really begin to discover more of who we are and our cosmic purpose.

As a final word, please don't dread or worry about any transit. I know that social media and the press sometimes likes to dramatise certain things in astrology and paint a pretty gloomy picture, but, honestly, these transits are here to help you to evolve and grow.

Saturn Return (28–30 Years Old)

Happening at around the age of 29, this is when Saturn returns back to the position it was in when you were born. This is an astrological rite of passage and usually brings a sense that everything in your life is beginning to crumble, fall apart and make absolutely no sense.

There may be a sudden break-up from the person you thought you'd spend the rest of your life with, or a realisation that you don't love the career you're in, or that you are no longer resonating with your friendship group or the way you spend your free time, and you begin to question who you are, what you want and what it's all about.

This is a huge transitional period when Saturn, the planet of structures and foundations, asks you whether this is the kind of relationship or career you want to be in for the rest of your life and pushes you to begin to break away from what's been expected of you for so long. This is the time when you can begin to grow into your true self and your full purpose and potential – when you begin to lay the foundations for who you're going to be and what the rest of your life is going to be about.

Anything happening during your Saturn return is to help you to grow, evolve and claim authority over your own life. It's helping you to overcome fears, face challenges, do the brave and scary thing, take responsibility for yourself and your life path, and know who you are. It will shake the foundations of your life, toppling all that you thought was safe and certain. But, on the other side, you and your life will never be the same again, for the better.

We will go through a second Saturn return in our late fifties, bringing the stereotypical 'midlife crisis'. After establishing yourself and your foundations in life and being responsible, you're now asked to look at the wisdom and lessons you've learned through your life and whether you're truly living your purpose. This is likely to coincide with big events, such as children leaving home, grandchildren arriving and retirement looming, and asks you to once again look at where you are in your life and make some meaningful changes to the structures and foundations that you've built your life upon.

There will be a third Saturn return in your late eighties when you reflect on your life and pass your wisdom and teachings down to others. It's a time of contemplating your life and legacy and what it was all about.

Three ways to make your Saturn return period easier:

1. Trust that, when it all seems to be falling apart, it's actually coming together.
2. Use this time to get clear on your values, boundaries and really get to know yourself.
3. Take responsibility for your life and what you want from your future.

Nodal Return (36 Years Old)

We talked about your lunar nodes in the last chapter; now, let's look at your nodal return. This is when the lunar nodes return back to the sign they were in when you were born. This brings a powerful period where you are invited to step on to the next path that your soul wants to journey along. This is a timeline shift in your life, if you choose to take it, that moves you into what's next for you.

Depending on how aligned you already are with the pathway of your soul, you may be pushed by challenging occurrences in your life to begin to move closer towards your north node destiny and move beyond those of your south node. This can be a time of immense soul growth where your pathway forward will become much clearer.

The more you move in the direction of your destiny and embrace your north node qualities, even if it feels uncomfortable and scary, the more things in your life will start to fall into place. This also means letting go of your south node qualities and moving beyond your comfort zone. The more you avoid this process and resist where you are being called to go, the more painful and difficult your life will become.

You have a nodal return every 18/19 years, and so your first one will come at 18 when you are coming into adulthood and stepping out into the world and then at 36, 54, and so on.

Halfway between your nodal return you will experience a reverse nodal return. This is when the lunar nodes are exactly opposite your own and serve as a check-in of whether you're on the right path. This is a time to fully explore your south node qualities and to learn from all of the positive aspects and integrate this wisdom to help you move forwards.

This is a good time to be honest about where you resist change and to look at your preferences, habits, beliefs systems and thought patterns, and whether they serve you or keep you in your comfort zone. This is a time to look at how far you have come and find closure on the past so that you can get to your future.

Three ways to make your nodal return period easier:

1. Look at repeating patterns in your life that aren't serving you and move beyond them.
2. Consider where you are being challenged to grow and rise and move towards more purpose.
3. Notice where you are resisting life and step out of your comfort zone.

Pluto Square (36–42 Years Old)

Any Pluto transits are life-changing, but, very often, they are some of the hardest to navigate as Pluto takes you deep into transformation. I often describe Pluto as a wrecking ball and, as the planet of death, rebirth and transformation, Pluto takes us through this process in all the ways that we need to be taken through it for our soul's evolution and awakening. Pluto takes us into our deepest truth and power, and asks us to confront what is holding us back.

As Pluto has such a long orbit (248 years), not everyone will experience that many Pluto aspects; this will depend on your own chart. But we will all experience a Pluto square sometime in our late thirties/early forties (for some, this could be later in life due to Pluto's irregular transit). This is when Pluto is ninety degrees or three signs away from where it was when you were born.

This is a time of deep transformation and transmutation and discovering who you truly are. During this time, you're going to need to confront your shadows and subconscious fears, let go of your ego's plan in favour of that of your soul, and face all those things in your life that you have been avoiding. This can feel like an ego death as your sense of identity is tested and all that is not truly you or in alignment with your soul's path needs to be surrendered. This is truly an initiation and turning point in your life and, although this may feel like a breakdown, it's a breakthrough. It's to help you to find faith in you, your journey and your soul, and to connect with your true source of power and potential.

Three ways to make your Pluto square period easier:

1. Be honest about where you have been avoiding facing or dealing with certain things in your life. Use this time to claim back your power.
2. Look at where you are out of alignment with yourself and your soul, and where you have put your dreams and desires to one side.
3. Surrender to the process and embrace the transformation.

Neptune Square (39–41 Years Old)

When Neptune reaches ninety degrees or three signs away from where it was when you were born, you will experience your Neptune square. This can be a time of disillusionment, uncertainty and confusion as you wonder how you got here in your life and what it's all about, especially if you have strayed a long way away from your soul.

This is where you begin to untangle all the 'should's about your life and confront what you thought life was supposed to look like.

Your sense of self may be brought into question, and this is a beautiful time to be kind and gentle and really get to know your true self.

This can be a time of great spiritual awakening as you begin to yearn for a deeper connection with something greater, more meaning and purpose in your life and to follow some of your long-abandoned dreams. This is a time to surrender to your higher self and trust the unknown and the unfolding of your journey, as hard as that may feel.

Three ways to make your Neptune square period easier:

1. Become your own best friend and use this time to truly deeply know and understand yourself.
2. Avoid escapism and instead use this time for deep reflection and spiritual connection.
3. Begin to pursue dreams and desires and what is alive within you.

Uranus Opposition (39–42 Years Old)

Just when you think that you have life all figured out, Uranus, the planet of liberation, freedom and awakening, comes in to shake things up. Sometime in your late thirties/early forties, Uranus reaches a point where it's directly opposite where it was when you were born. This brings a spiritual wake-up call where Uranus asks you if you're living an authentic life that's true to you and in alignment with your soul.

If you've been doing the inner work and you're spiritually fulfilled and connected to your higher source of power, allowing that to guide you, this can be an exciting time when Uranus pushes you into a life of even more meaning and purpose.

If you've been ignoring your inner niggles, living a life that doesn't fulfil you and staying stuck in relationships, work or situations that restrict, stifle and shrink you, you're going to know about it. Uranus will tip your life upside down in order to get you to pay attention and listen and get back on track. It's going to liberate and free you from all that keeps you from being all of you and fulfilling your soul contracts in this lifetime.

There will be a sudden feeling that you're running out of time and a period of questioning everything about your life. You'll start to look at what you haven't accomplished, where you haven't lived up to your potential, followed your purpose and lived life on your own terms. You may find yourself questioning your worth, feeling inadequate and disconnected from who you truly are – and this is a wake-up call to connect back to your spiritual self and begin to live a life of meaning and purpose.

Three ways to make your Uranus opposition period easier:

1. Reconnect to your true authentic self and who you were before the world told you who to be. Set your inner rebel free.
2. Reconnect to your full potential and purpose. Follow what inspires you and brings you to life.
3. Make changes in your life and break free from what feels stifling and restrictive.

Chiron Return (49–50 Years Old)

Chiron is known as the wounded healer and represents the traumas and wounds that you carry with you through your life, showing you where healing, lessons and growth need to take place and how you can transform your healing into wisdom to help others.

When you're around 50 years old, Chiron returns back to the position it was in when you were born and helps you to heal and release pain from your past and alchemise this pain into purpose. This can be a challenging and painful process as you are called to face the consequences of your past choices and anything in your life that still needs healing. Things that you have been avoiding dealing with will come back around to be processed and you'll be able to clearly see the core woundings that have kept you repeating patterns and cycles in your life. This may be a time of deep insecurities, but profound healing of these things that may have been a theme through your whole life.

With all of this comes a transformative opportunity to take back your power and free yourself from old fears, wounds and pain. This is a time of deep spiritual awakening where you get to understand why you have been through what you have been through, what it's taught you and how it's made you who you are. And now you will be given a second chance to become who you want to be, taking all that you now know and making changes to align with more of your true soul self and live the life you want to live. There is also a deep understanding of how you can now take these life experiences and help others who are going through similar situations.

Three ways to make your Chiron return period easier:

1. Find the wisdom in your wounds and the purpose in your pain. Alchemise your past into potential for the future.
2. Forgive yourself and others. Realise that you were doing the best you could with what you knew. Commit to doing things differently going forwards.

3. Look at what is still unhealed in your life and take a healing journey, with professional support and help if need be. It's time to heal and free yourself.

I truly hope this part has helped you to realise how astrology can give you so much guidance and insight into your cosmic purpose. Take your time to learn more about your own chart and seek the help of a professional to read your chart and give you the exact timings of your transits and so much more if this calls to you.

FINAL WORDS

My love, thank you so much for taking this journey with me and allowing me to be your soul guide.

As I mentioned at the beginning of this book, this is not an easy journey, so well done for being brave, vulnerable and willing to truly look at yourself. I hope that through these pages you have started to know, trust, understand, accept and love yourself in new ways and, most of all, realise that you are a soul having a human experience and can connect back to your soul.

When you begin to allow your soul to live and experience life through you, when you know deep in your bones that you are always being supported and guided and when you remember how immensely powerful you are, life changes. You take back control over your own life, live in full trust, show up as more of you and go after your soul's desires. You see every experience, lesson and even hardships as opportunities for deeper growth, and you start to listen to and follow the whispers and nudges from your deep intuition, allowing yourself to be guided through life. And through all of this, you begin to understand that you have a cosmic purpose here on earth at this time and you start to live in this way.

I wish all of this for you. I truly hope that you have remembered how magical, special, perfect, whole and complete you are just by being you. And I hope that you allow your unique soul essence and vibration to begin to radiate out into the world so that we can see you, feel you, know you and be inspired by you.

You are the entire universe in a human body. You are stardust – don't ever forget that. And, if you do, go within, let your soul whisper to you and remind you that you are infinite, expansive and all-knowing.

Remember, too, that this is just the very beginning of your journey, and your journey itself is part of your cosmic purpose. Take your time, fully experience it all, follow the signs and allow it to unfold. In doing so, you will discover even more magic, purpose and potential than you had ever even imagined.

I always love to hear from you, so please share your journey towards your cosmic purpose, tagging me on Instagram @kirsty_gallagher_.

ENDNOTES

Chapter 5: You Must Realise Who You're Not

1 Davis, N., 5 Apr. 2023. 'Human memory may be unreliable after just a few seconds, scientists find.' *Guardian*. Retrieved from https://www.theguardian.com/science/2023/apr/05/short-term-memory-illusions-study; Henry, L., 1 Dec. 2022. 'Is memory reliable?' *The Classic Journal*. Retrieved from https://theclassicjournal.uga.edu/index.php/2022/12/01/is-memory-reliable/.

Chapter 14: Face Your Fears

1 Gillihan, S. J., 19 Jul. 2019. 'How often do your worries actually come true?' *Psychology Today*. Retrieved from https://www.psychologytoday.com/intl/blog/think-act-be/201907/how-often-do-your-worries-actually-come-true?amp.

ACKNOWLEDGEMENTS

To my wonderful family: Sandra, Kylie, Kerry, Liam, Stephanie, Soraya, Jake, Chloe, Edward, Isaac and my late Grandpa Donald. I love you all and thank you for always loving and supporting me.

To Sam, you're my person, always. Thank you for being you, walking alongside me and for your endless support and encouragement. I love you. And so much love to my godson Harley (even though he calls me the bloody witch!) and Welsh family.

Aunty Mabel, as this book comes out on what would have been your 108th birthday, I know that you are still with me, teaching and guiding me. Sharon, your light still illuminates my way forward and I am so grateful that you sent Sam to me straight after your passing; she's taken such good care of me for you. I am blessed to have had two such incredible teachers in my life and hope that I am doing you both proud.

Holly Whitaker, I love making books with you. Thank you for always believing in me. Special mentions to Anna Bowen and Anya Hayes for all your hard work and support, and to Mylène Mozas-Sauvignon for creating such a beautiful front cover.

To my editor, Julia Kellaway, thank you for such thoughtful and helpful edits and for making the process easy and enjoyable.

Thank you to Fearne Cotton (and your brilliant family) for your friendship and support and to Happy Place for having me as part of the family. I love contributing to the app and festivals and now making books with you too.

Thank you to Chris Evans, Tash and family for your friendship and support and for being you – I absolutely adore you. And to everyone on the *Virgin Breakfast Show* and CarFest team, thank you for allowing me to share the moon magic and my work with the nation. I love you all.

Craig David, thank you so much for all of your love, good vibes and support with this book. You helped more than you will even know in bringing this book into the world. I appreciate you so much. Here's to walking through open doors and believing in impossible things. It's glow-up time!

Luisa Bradshaw White (you are so fu**ing powerful), thank you for coming back into my life after so many other lifetimes together; I love doing life with you.

Louise Carron Harris, I cannot wait for more Glastonbury and earth grid adventures together and solving the world sofa times! Adore you, soul sister.

Becki Rabin, from those girls living together in 'the church' to now, we've been through so many life changes, but our friendship has never changed.

Lisa Strong, I love all the versions of each other we have known over the last few decades. Here's to more White Isle and worldwide adventures together.

Rebecca Dennis, my dragon sister. I love how we weave and walk each other through life, side by side.

Soulla Demetriou, from Costa Rica to Ibiza and many lifetimes before, I appreciate you and our friendship and magical times together.

Angharad Owen, you came into my life at just the right time, and I thank you for all of your healing and magic. I can't wait to see where we go together.

Valesca, thank you for holding me through my dark night of the soul and beyond.

To my Lunar Living online sisterhood and Mystery School Coven, thank you for all your support, lunar love and for being the best sisterhood ever. My never-ending gratitude to my right-hand woman Helen Elias; nothing I do would be what it is without you.

Thank you to everyone in my IG and online community. You are the most supportive and magical community ever. Thank you for continuing to show up for yourself and each other. Remember, you are never alone, you've got this, I've got you, we've got each other. We're only just getting started and there is so much yet to come.

If you are holding this book in your hands, thank you for allowing me to be your guide and I truly hope that this book has helped you to remember who you truly are and uncover Your Cosmic Purpose.

Thanks, too, to *This Morning*, and everyone who has invited me on your podcasts or lives to share my work. Thank you to Zoe and Morgan for your magical jewellery, Ancient and Brave for your support and incredible products, and Sacred for the beautiful collaborations.

So much love and gratitude to these special people in my life, you know who you are and what you do: Rangan and Vidh Chatterje, Brett Waters, Caggie Dunlop, Ian Steed and Julie Morrow.

If I have not named you, it's not because you are forgotten or that I am not grateful. It's simply that I have been blessed to have so many wonderful people touch my life and not enough pages left to mention you all – it would be another book in itself! If you have ever been a part of my life in any way, thank you.

ABOUT THE AUTHOR

Photo © Alexandra Cameron

Kirsty Gallagher, the UK's leading voice in spirituality, astrology, lunar living and soul-led personal development, is a multi-*Sunday Times* bestselling author, sought-after speaker, host of the UK's No.1 spirituality podcast and founder of Soul Emporium.

Renowned worldwide for her unmatched knowledge and wisdom, Kirsty brings lunar cycles, astrology and ancient spiritual wisdom into the modern world in a practical, accessible way. Through her books, podcast, workshops and courses, she has helped millions globally reconnect with ancient wisdom, live in flow with natural cycles and weave the magic of astrology, divine feminine energy, seasonal living, crystals, meditation and yoga into their daily lives – unlocking deep transformation.

Her mission is simple yet profound: to help people align with the rhythms of the universe, reconnect with their soul's potential and purpose, and create a life of greater flow, success, and joy.

Kirsty is the author of the *Sunday Times* bestsellers, *Lunar Living* and *The Goddess Path*, as well as the much-loved *Lunar Living Journal*, *Sacred Seasons* and *Crystals for Self-Care*. She also hosts *The Kirsty Gallagher Podcast*, the UK's No.1 spirituality podcast, where she shares weekly 'Cosmic Weather Reports', 'Monday Meditations' and empowering spiritual guidance.

For over 20 years, Kirsty has shared her inspiring words at more than 80 retreats worldwide and led hundreds of sell-out workshops, corporate talks and branded events. Her wisdom has been featured in *ELLE*, *Harper's Bazaar*, *Glamour*, *The Sunday Times*, *YOU*, *Red*, *Stylist*, *Good Housekeeping*, *Marie Claire*, *This Morning*, *The Chris Evans Breakfast Show* and more.

She is also the founder of Lunar Living – an online membership connecting women worldwide in a sisterhood dedicated to living in harmony with the moon's cycles – and Soul Emporium, a soul-infused marketplace for crystals and self-care.

Kirsty's work has touched the lives of millions, building one of the most engaged and connected spiritual communities, with over half a million like-minded souls following her journey. Her words are often described as a 'warm cup of tea' or a 'comforting hug', offering guidance, clarity and reassurance in a way that feels both deeply personal and profoundly transformative to many. Through her down-to-earth wisdom and heartfelt delivery, she creates a space where people feel truly seen, supported and inspired.

Find out more at kirstygallagher.com or join her Instagram community at @kirsty_gallagher_